WITHIN THREE MINDS
Common Sense Psychology

Library

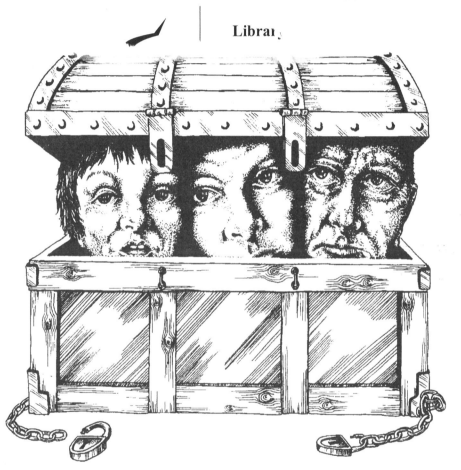

By

Dr. DAVID BUCHAN

First published in the UK by

SOSM Publishing
PO BOX 56
SWINDON
SN5 6LT

ISBN 0 9533020 1 6

A CIP record for this book is available from the British Library

Distributed by SOSM Publishing

First published in Workbook format in 1998. Copyright © 1998 David Buchan

1999 Limited Edition

DAVID BUCHAN

Within Three Minds

SOSM Publishing 1999

ACKNOWLEDGEMENTS

Frank James has been nagging me for a couple of years now, to complete a book about Stress Management. Several hundred pages in and lots of help from Frank, it was already too large to be practical when I stalled on the psychology of Stress. Originally, in an attempt to keep the book manageable I had only allocated fifty pages for both the subject **and** the solutions.* Since then Frank continued to nag, I continued to stall. In January 1998 I said I would finally "write **the** book" [what I hadn't mentioned was the book would be Within Three Minds (W3M™)]. In August I gave Frank two weeks to produce the illustrations for W3M™. Despite the very short time limits, being given some pretty vague briefs/ specifications and that the book wasn't the one he was expecting; Frank came up with the goods. Thanks Frank for the much appreciated support, advice, nagging, the illustrations and your friendship.

I would also like to take this opportunity to thank my partner Lesley for her support.

A lot of other people that can't be named, are of course the thousands of clients that had my version of Transactional Analysis (TA) thrown at them and the very unique clients that unknowingly gave me the insights/ new concepts of TA. Thank you.

*The Workbook edition of W3M™ was in print by November 1998. Although not specifically the psychology of Stress, W3M™ is the part I stalled on. Even with almost two hundred pages all I could cover was the subject, it will take another two hundred pages to cover the solutions!

WITHIN THREE MINDS

Imagine a world where there is no war, no depression, little illness, where people are actually happy [as opposed to existing from day to day]. Neighbours are friendly, interested and not only have time for you, but will actually go out of their way to help you. Crime, poverty, hunger, drug abuse are almost unheard of.

That was intended to be the world you live in now!

In the 1960's a revolutionary psychology named Transactional Analysis (TA) was created/ discovered that had the potential to actually eradicate almost all of societies ailments.

Unfortunately most of societies ailments bring in big money, mainly for "academics". [Basically the higher your education the greater your opportunity to make money. You could make better/ smarter weapons, offer drugs/ "cures" for physical illnesses, design more effective ways to make consumers part with their very hard earned cash, etc. The more skilful you are at this the more you earn! If you couldn't improve on these issues, you can make just as much money by inventing/ creating even more types of misery and pain! If you don't have wars, plagues, pestilence, and pain; you don't earn big money!!]

The original intent of Transactional Analysis was to teach the average person in the street how to improve their lives. It was a wonderful positive time bomb. When enough people understood and used TA the world would begin to right itself and people could enjoy every aspect of their lives. Obviously optimum improvement would take a few generations; but an immediate improvement could be felt now!

Unfortunately Psychological Groups and academia took TA under their wing, telling people such rubbish as "you can't use it, unless you're qualified", "it's too complicated for the average person", "you need years of training before you can use it", "it's good in theory but it has no practical value", etc. At this point academia *did* make it too complicated to be useful. What a surprise the people who earn the most from misery and pain; kept the knowledge of how to avoid that misery and pain, **secret**. These people stole *your* birthright, *your* happiness, out of greed.

This book holds the secrets they stole, read it and weep!

Transactional Analysis is unique in that simple/ basic/ recognisable terms are used to explain each aspect of the human condition and mind.

Even the title becomes simple with a little thought: - "Transactional Analysis"; people constantly interact with other people. These interactions called transactions, involved a hidden [unconscious] exchange of energy called *Strokes* [the unconscious mind uses Strokes as life energy, we begin to die without them.] Transaction-al Analysis is the analysis [the recognition and understanding], of transactions.

Obviously if we can die without enough *Strokes,* it's pretty important to find out how we get them and how we lose them.

Everything was kept as simple as possible; just glancing through the list of contents you see chapters such as: -

Parent, Adult and Child

Strokes

Game Playing

Stamp Collecting

Scripts

Each one of these terms is simple and easy to use; very roughly if you think or behave like a Parent ["**where** have you been?", "**who** said you could do that?", "**what** do you think you are doing!", etc.], you are in your Parent mind. The Parent, Adult and Child are the three-parts/ minds of our consciousness.

If you think or behave like a young child ["I want", "it's mine", "I hate you!", "its not fair!", etc.], you are in your Child mind.

If you are calm, logical, reasonable, you are behaving as people may wish to behave as adults, therefore you are in your Adult mind.

Strokes begin as an actual touch; therefore if you are physically being stroked you are receiving Strokes!

If you are Game Playing, you are unconsciously playing games, some complicated, some simple, each "player" taking turns until there is a winner.

If you are Stamp Collecting, you are literally collecting "Stamps", different values, different sizes, each person having their favourite type. Professionals have big stamp collections, lots of albums, and trade stamps regularly. Amateurs have little collections, perhaps only a couple of albums, but plenty of interest. Beginners sometimes just collect anything, even accepting bargain packages of stamps and albums, that no-one else wants.

A script is the text/ direction for a play or film. If you are using a script, you are following the directions and words from the script. Again like Stamp Collecting some people follow the script like school children in a school play, some as if they were in amateur dramatics, and some people follow the script as hardened professionals: totally plausible and totally committed.

TA really was just as simple as this; I have returned to these simple ideas and understandable language in writing this book. However this is still a psychology, so it requires a little bit of effort from you.

After all, you didn't expect to receive **the secrets of life** without *some work*?

Every aspect of human behaviour can be explained through Transactional Analysis.

Transactional Analysis can explain **any** part of the human condition that you may find yourself in, whether it is anxiety, depression, relationship problems, suicidal, addictive behaviour, dietary disorders, stress, bad habits, destructive behaviour, etc.

Including the astounding idea that we **did not evolve as human beings** in the traditional sense! [Psychologists have known this for decades but kept it secret from the general public.]

LIST OF CONTENTS

Page no.

How to read this book?   5

The Parent, Adult and Child   7

Mammalian Minds   40

Strokes   49

Life Positions   61

Game Playing   70

Pleasure   78

Scripts   88

Stamp Collecting   119

Frames of Reference   135

Points of Commitment   142

Needs   159

Conclusion   163

Glossary   172

Moments   178

HOW TO READ THIS BOOK

This section may seem strange, since you may have been reading books for years perhaps decades. This book will give you a completely new understanding of yourself and the people around you. Just one skipped word could change the structure of this book. As such you would begin to interpret the information [reading it as you see it], rather than understand and accept the information as it is written.

Even reading as carefully as possible you may still find that understanding comes later, rather than whilst you read each piece. This is perfectly normal and not something to worry about, but it is something to be prepared for!

Please read the entire book from front to back as quickly as you are comfortable with; then, having completed the book, please return to each chapter that you wish to read more thoroughly and take your time. One of the reasons for this, is that whilst each chapter appears complete in it's own right, you need the background knowledge to implement and understand each chapter.

As a first time reader you will almost certainly need the Glossary. It may be useful to place a small post-it note/ bookmark at the beginning of the Glossary so that you can refer to it easily without interrupting your flow of thought or understanding of the section you are reading.

As you read the book, you are likely to have "wow! / Yes!" moments.

These are moments when a sudden flash of realisation or understanding comes to mind [enlightenment]; perhaps when you suddenly realise or understand why something has occurred in the past, or maybe a difficulty that is occurring in your present life. A spare post-it note/ bookmark would be useful at this point so that you may mark this section for re-reading.

It should be noted at this point that the contents of this book are primarily designed so that you may understand yourself and your behaviour/ actions/ feelings/ thoughts.

This will allow you to become self aware and self responsible for your future well being.

Often in just understanding that the things you may have suffered from, have a common theme and are/ or have been suffered by others will bring some comfort. It is therefore important that you <u>understand</u> the contents of this book before you use them. If you come across a word or phrase that you do not understand go to the Glossary and continue re-reading that entire section until it makes sense.

It is also important to note that common words have been used that have a second or different meaning to the usual or accepted use.
i.e. Parent mind, you do not need to be a parent to have and use your Parent mind. All references to Parent mind/ Parental have been given a capital initial to help you recognise that the book is not referring to the word "parent" which as you can see has been given a lower case "p".

Some typefaces may be different, whilst some areas have italics.

Italics are usually used to indicate or elaborate on a significant point.

Whilst different typefaces may be used to indicate peripheral information of interest to students and/ or readers that already have an interest in Transactional Analysis.

As a first time reader, if you find information in the sections with a different typeface [such as this] distracting, feel free to ignore them.

Where I have introduced a new typeface that it is important for you to read, the first few times you come across it I will ask you to:- "Please read this".

If you are reading this particular paragraph, you have one of a **limited** edition. This particular edition has a different binding, cover and a slightly different text to the "Workbook" edition. It is limited to a print run of three thousand books. As several books are required for the legal depositories and academic libraries there slightly less than three thousand books available to the general public.

THE PARENT, ADULT AND CHILD

Within Three Minds is loosely based on the structure of Transactional Analysis. Transactional Analysis works with the premise that each individual has three conscious minds. The minds are nicknamed the Child, Parent and Adult.

Very roughly, the Child mind is created by and can be recognised through our receipt of feelings usually pain and pleasure. The Parent mind is recognised through behaviour and actions that mimic the perceived behaviour of our true parents or other significant adults. The Adult is a rational logical mind that behaves in a way that we would like to behave as reasoning adults.

As with all forms of psychology this process is based on theory and theories constantly change. Therefore differences of opinion between Transactional Analysts and Practitioners using this particular psychology will occur. One of the primary differences is the awareness and acceptance that intense anger is in the domain of the Parent, and not as has previously been suggested in earlier publications, in the Child mind. Anger that may be recognised as temper [or foot-stamping] is still in the domain of the Child.

Additionally, whilst the Child and Parent minds are referred to as conscious, they more reasonably mimic an iceberg, where the tip of the iceberg i.e. that which is above water is the conscious mind and the submerged portion is the unconscious. The tip of the iceberg is constantly changing, so that at any one time there is more or less access to a conscious portion of the Child or Parent (This will be dealt with in more depth later).

Activities within the Child and Parent are occasionally referred to as "React"/ "Reacting"/ "Reaction". These terms are used to explain the difference between the normal day to day responses in the Child and Parent, and when a survival response occurs within the Child and Parent (Reaction).

When a perceived threat to our survival is identified, we react with a Fight or Flight response; Fight being Parental, Flight being Child. Depending on the severity of this perceived threat, the "iceberg" may submerge completely, therefore we have no conscious ability to recognise or override this fight/ flight reaction.

"Additionally, whilst the Child and Parent minds are referred to as conscious, they more reasonably mimic an iceberg…"

Iceberg illustrated by Frank James.

A practitioner himself, Frank portrays "Jungian" symbolism/ hidden meaning in many of his illustrations.

These are fairly obvious in this particular illustration since the entire scene represents the psyche, including the "light of consciousness and the Shadow". The Ocean/ Sea is deliberately portrayed dark for the inner depths of the subconscious. Representing dark desires from the depths, the total blackness of repression and the subconscious itself. Stormy weather is indicative of consciousness since our conscious thoughts [and lives] rarely run smoothly, being constantly affected by our emotions.

Even the revealed portion of the iceberg/ cliffs are riddled with the dark of the "Shadow". And of course the icebergs/ clouds/ consciousness doesn't exist since they are a reality created from illusion [Frank's artwork] and your consciousness. [If you look carefully you may notice that the icebergs are not drawn, but suggested/ outlined through a collection of lines and gaps.]

Some of Frank's illustrations are psychologically innocent, whilst others carry deeper issues and meaning. [Identifying the underlying meaning, will give a good insight into your own mind!] Think about this illustration: until it was pointed out, you may have *thought* you **saw** icebergs or cliffs, but your mind actually created them!

Throughout this book, as with traditional Transactional Analysis (TA), the Child, Parent and Adult will have an initial capital letter to differentiate between the ego state (i.e. the mind) and an actual child, parent or adult. The Child, Parent and Adult are referred to as minds/ ego states in that each of these minds have their own behaviour patterns, thoughts, actions and experiences.

By/ through understanding of the three minds sets them free. Just by trying to understand which mind is which and how they work, strengthens the Adult mind. Even partial understanding of the three minds allows us to begin to *balance* the minds appropriately. It is not a case of which mind we should all strive to be in; but rather a healthy balance so that the needs of each mind are met safely and enjoyably. We need time where we are truly Adult [rational, logical and understanding], where we are Parental [carrying out mundane tasks efficiently, travelling through life's tasks easily and with little thought.] and where we are in our Child mind [enjoying pleasure, exploring what we *want*, and having fun].

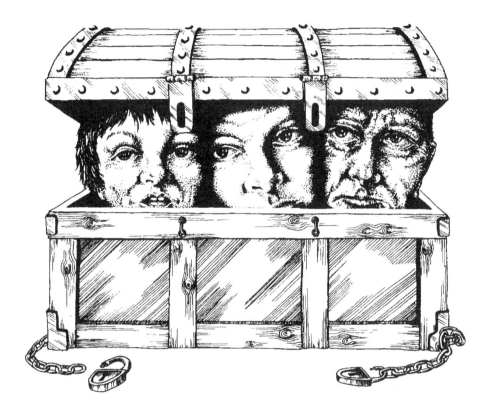

"…. understanding of the three minds sets them free."

Like Pandora's box; by reading this book you let out all sorts of new things that cannot be returned. However, if you do not know the contents of the box, then you cannot control your own destiny!

THE CHILD

The Child mind is a primary/ mammalian mind that we are born with. It is created by identifying a level or intensity of pain or pleasure connected to everything that we experience and/ or observe within our first few years of life.

Although the Child behaves and very much remains as a five year old, it is still possible to continue adding new information to the Child. However, unlike the first few years of life where data is stored through direct experience and observation, later information usually has to be added either through major physiological changes or with the permission of the Adult. i.e. Puberty brings a whole new series of pleasurable experiences whilst adolescence often brings a whole new series of painful experiences (Angst).

The Child mind is created by attributing *feelings* during the first few years of life in connection to everything that it observes or experiences directly. [Approximately the first five to six years of life.] These can be pleasurable or painful. *

It is generally accepted that the young individual recognises two primary types of emotion these being pain or pleasure. However, the ability to recognise different intensities of pain or pleasure is almost infinitesimal. In adult life, these different intensities are often given titles i.e. Bereavement, Shame, Guilt, etc.

It should be recognised that these are still types and intensities of pain rather than individual feelings in their own right. As such everyone experiences Bereavement in an individual way with a unique [for that person] intensity. The same generally holds true for most of the named feelings i.e. grief, guilt, etc.

For the purpose of this book, it is assumed that the Child mind is directly connected to the Limbic and autonomic nervous system. As such, it is a perfectly acceptable survival trait to identify that which is painful, and that, which is pleasurable.

The identification of intensities of emotion allow us two additional skills:-

1. A pain/ pain choice would be impossible to choose without an awareness [this may be conscious or unconscious, the awareness may be purely in terms of the survival of the organism. Therefore the *choice* may be carried out in the unconscious Child] of which was most painful.

2. Once the intensity of pain can be established, this is directly equal to the intensity of effort needed to avoid that, which is painful.

Similarly, the process is equal for pleasure, since if you know how pleasurable something is, you also know how much effort to put in to achieve it.

This is a *mammalian* process, since part of mammalian development is to identify optimum survival skills. The process is identical in the Child and Parent. [see Mammalian Minds at the end of this chapter.]

Generally this process serves us well but it should be noted that young children experience pain and pleasure at a much higher intensity than adults do. Therefore an experience that an adult may shrug off, can create such a level of intensity in a child that it must be avoided (pain) or pursued (pleasure) at all costs. This often leads to phobia (pain) or irrational/ immoral behaviour (pleasure) in adult life.

*NB the Child mind is created by how we **feel** and not by how we think.*

Often in early childhood, children *feel* bloody awful: -

"**Don't** do that…., tell me **later**…., **Not** now!…, **No**!…, **Go** and play".

The emotional damage caused to the child during this period may [if not addressed through the Adult mind, later in life.] be permanent.

Whenever a person is in the Child mind they have all the analytical ability of a five-year-old. People in their Child mind require reassurance, may expect punishment, can be playful, and are occasionally vindictive.

*When we **react** in the Child mind the driving process __always__ responds to the feeling prevalent at that time.*

i.e. If anxious or fearful the reaction will be the __Flight__ response in stress, if amorous then a sexual reaction will occur, if hungry then a deep desire/ reaction to eat will occur. Where we are unconsciously __driven__ to run away, __driven__ to mate, __driven__ to eat, etc. All of the __feelings__ and thoughts [if any] are focused entirely on meeting that particular driving need.

There is little if any rational thought; where there is, it is usually devoted entirely to achieving our desire/ need.

NB. True rational thought process is purely the domain of the Adult mind and will be discussed later in this chapter.

This causes several problems, in that the Child mind is very much a black or white mind. As far as the Child is concerned, things are either right or wrong. There are no grey areas. This often causes problems because of the limited rational capability of the Child.

The Child will usually come to conclusions based on feeling and what is observed, rather than using conscious logical thought processes. E.g. a Child that is taught that Father Christmas will not bring them a present if they are naughty; then finds that they have not received the present they expected can only come to the conclusion that they are *bad*.

Even a tiny percentage of doubt can lead to the misperception within the Child that it is bad. I.e. if one is perceived as ninety-percent good and ten-percent bad, where the ten-percent bad cannot be improved upon, the Child will gradually perceive that the only solution is to accept that it [the Child] is bad. This is often compounded by qualifying statements where the Child perceives that it is good *if* …. Ultimately whatever the qualifying statement (if …..) is; if it is not achievable or if it meets the ninety percent/ ten percent rule the child will ultimately return to the easiest black and white conclusion. I.e. if it is good when it behaves, yet is aware that it occasionally does not behave, it [the Child] is therefore bad and will accept this as part of it's programming.

If the Child constantly perceives that it is *bad*, it may come to the conclusion that it is unlovable. Ultimately this will reduce to the easiest conclusion this being that they are unloved.

In Dr Thomas Harris's work (I'm OK, You're OK, 1970), where the Child perceives it is unloved "it adopts the not OK position". In fact, Dr. Harris states that everyone adopts the "not OK" position within the Child. My own clinical practice (over 10,000 hours of one to one work) supports this, since I have only come across one person that may not have adopted the Not OK position.

[This particular client attended for a very short time therefore a full assessment wasn't possible. However it should be noted that by its very nature clinical practice attracts Not OK people, as such a comparison with people without the need for therapeutic assistance has not been carried out.]

Personally I would suggest that *most* people adopt a not OK position.

It should also be noted that the identification of being unloved/ not OK, is **relative**. Where at the light end of the scale, one may merely perceive that one's parents did not have time for them, whilst at the other extreme one may perceive that one's parents actively disliked or hated them. Obviously most people are somewhere in the middle.

*The perception that we **feel** unloved is usually **repressed**.*

Therefore it is fairly rare to discover someone who clearly recognises that one or both or their parents didn't love them when they were children. Many teenagers *feel* that their parents' affection is limited or conditional; yet continue to repress the evidence that they feel unloved.

Feeling unloved is a condition that affects the choices and actions from within the Child for the **rest of our lives,** if not identified and addressed. Whilst there are many other things (strokes, scripts, drivers etc.*) that affect our behaviour most of them are coloured or connected by this primary *misperception*. It should be noted that it is usually a misperception in that the recognition of being loved or unloved has nothing to do with the parents intent. In fact ironically the more the parents love their children, the more likely they are to create the misperception within each Child/ child [this affects the young child and the Child mind] that they are unloved. This will be explained in more depth through the development of the Parent and Adult.

*See Glossary.

14

The Child mind is essential for every day life. *Everything* that we feel we want and therefore choose is decided by the Child mind.

Obviously, this is something that we should be aware of since regardless of our actual age, the Child retains the age and behaves as a five year old, therefore making the choices that a five year old would make regardless of the circumstances. i.e. Whilst the intent is to choose a new <u>lover</u> the Child may lead us to choose a replacement Mother or Father. Obviously there is going to be a serious conflict of interest at some point in the new relationship.

Usually the entire process of choice is unconscious; however the intent of this book is to allow you to become conscious of these choices and decisions and therefore come to a compromise between all three minds rather than allowing the Child to give us inappropriate desires/ behaviour.

Obviously **regardless of conscious awareness, the Child mind will still identify that which we want**; although conscious awareness *may* allow us a true choice more suitable for an adult situation.
E.g. you have just sufficient funds in your bank account to pay your fuel bill. On your journey to the Gas Company you pass your favourite shop. On looking inside you see something you have 'always wanted'. At this point, the Child mind working on its own will lead you to spend your funds on whatever it is you have always wanted. To help you to do this, it may lead you to *forget* about or ignore the Gas bill. However, if you have a conscious awareness of how the Child mind behaves, you can choose to over-ride this particular desire and therefore meet your a/ Adult commitments.

Whilst this is a very obvious example, it should be noted that more subtle coercion by the Child is the norm. In fact, boredom and inattention are some of the weapons used by the Child in an attempt to either achieve its desires or demonstrate that its needs are not being met. Intense emotional charges are also used, often with devastating effect.

However with sufficient conscious awareness even these situations can be worked with.
Identification of threats is an unconscious task of the Child. As such, innocuous situations can elicit a 'flight' reaction within the Child. In the lighter stages of reacting, conscious awareness may be present.

However, it can rarely over-ride the Child reaction once the Flight response is triggered.

i.e. you suffer from arachnophobia. On seeing a small to medium sized spider, you react by becoming fearful. You may be able to mentally talk to yourself. "That it won't hurt you"; "That it is more frightened of you" etc. But you still <u>feel</u> fearful. However, if a <u>large</u> spider runs rapidly towards you, your Child reaction can be so severe that you run screaming from this spider. True conscious awareness is lost. Your ability to affect the Child response is zero!

You may not have recognised at this point that the Child and Parent are significant throughout all mammals. In fact, the Child and Parent are often nicknamed "The Mammalian Minds". Regardless of the mammal, dog, cat, rabbit, they all evidence Child and Parent minds. However for the purpose of this book, I would like you to think of these minds as the Survival Minds since the Child and Parent are directly responsible for every day survival.

As I mentioned earlier the Child and Parent minds are similar to icebergs where conscious awareness is in the upper tip and unconscious drives and desires are in the submerged portion.

When we are under stress the iceberg sinks deeper until we have little or no conscious awareness of our Child or Parent minds. And therefore are totally at the mercy of the unconscious need to survive. The Child mind is the flight side of "fight or flight"* in stress as such. We have a very powerful unconscious desire to escape or run away when the unconscious Child becomes aware of a perceived threat.

In a full Fight or Flight reaction, there is no longer any conscious thought process involved.

These issues cannot be run away from, wherever we go these issues go with us. The unconscious Child mind will continue to react until we are affected by/ suffer from stress. Warning Unfortunately many perceived threats to the unconscious Child are either emotional charges, the effects of heightened sensate awareness, poor thinking patterns, outside of our Frames of Reference (see glossary), or a reaction to psychological history [events from our past]. flags will be sent to the conscious mind, but not always in a form that the conscious mind would recognise.

*See Glossary.

This means that where a perceived threat cannot be run away from or escaped, the unconscious Child will anxiete or symptom. The symptoms can range from depression (psychological) to psoriasis (physiological).

When the perceived threat is removed, the symptoms normally go into remission. However, where the perceived threat remains, additional symptoms or anxiety are added to the original symptoms.

As a general rule, the unconscious mind is relatively lazy and will use the same symptom each time a particular level of stress occurs. This can often cause confusion, as the symptoms do not appear to have any obvious connection to the present stressors.
This is usually because an asthmatic attack at four years of age may have protected the young child from an arduous or unpleasant task. At forty years of age, the same symptom may be triggered off at the point that our children leave home. Although this is a completely different type of stressor, the original symptom is used throughout.

Where successful efforts have been made to overcome the asthma a new symptom may arise and will now be the first choice under any stressful situation. In addition, where the asthma has not been resolved and the Child mind still perceives it is under the original stressor (i.e. arduous or unpleasant task) it will design new symptoms for subsequent stressors whilst retaining the asthma. This is one of the reasons why people may present themselves to their medical doctor with a series of symptoms.
e.g. Asthma, psoriasis, irritable bowel and panic attacks, each one starting on a new date.

Even physiological conditions that originate from the Child in this manner will be alleviated when stress is removed or managed. It is relatively easy to identify where a physiological condition is inherent or psychologically triggered, by increasing the level of stress an individual perceives they are under. At this point the condition will be triggered off or get worse and will return to a natural level when the additional stress is removed.
Some people's natural level of stressor identification is sufficiently high to allow their anxiety/ symptoms to constantly affect them; therefore it is the *additional* symptoms that confirm a stress response. Common sense dictates that purely physical condition will continue to affect the person regardless of whether they are under any additional psychological pressure.

Whilst these conditions are often referred to as psychosomatic and often dismissed by other people, it should be noted that they are very real and very physical to the person suffering from them. Frames of Reference become subtly altered until every piece of data available to our Child mind becomes evidence to support our condition. Dwelling on a symptom even momentarily can actualise/ realise that symptom; in these circumstances just thinking about a symptom can create it. One of the tasks of the unconscious mind is to follow the instructions given to it through the conscious mind. Since the conscious mind is unaware that many of its thought processes are actually taken as commands, it is unable to avoid or prevent a gradual slide from thoughts (a psychological condition) to a physical condition. The awareness of an impending physical condition is again accepted as a command and will be followed by the unconscious mind.

We <u>literally</u> become what we think.

Things may be becoming confusing since only the Child has been discussed in detail so far; yet pain and pleasure, stress, fight or flight, symptoms, psychosomatic conditions, etc. have all been mentioned.

Are you in your Child mind when worrying? Are you constantly bad or unloved in the Child? Why is sex in the domain of the Child mind? Sex! This is something else to add to the confusion, how can sex be the domain of the Child, if the Child behaves like a five year old?

It is useful to think of the Child mind as a coin: one face being heads, one face being tails and an edge around the circumference.

In a healthy Child mind the "coin" would be on its edge. This is a neutral position being neither heads or tails. If the Child is becoming involved in something pleasurable then it will "fall" pleasure [tails] side up. If the Child is becoming involved in something potentially painful then it will "fall" pain [heads] side up.

As we move into the Adult or Parent minds, the Child can return to its neutral position.

Since the head of a coin is usually quite different from the tail, this represents the Child perfectly.

The pleasure face of the Child has different drives, attitudes, needs, emotions, chemicals/ hormones, etc. to the pain face. This can give the impression that it is two distinctly different creatures. But as a general rule when we pursue pleasure then only the pleasure face of the Child is seen. When we avoid pain the only the pain face is seen. NB the Child can swap between the pleasure and pain faces in less than a second.

Certain issues reside in particular sides of the Child, but these can be different for different people.

Sex is usually associated with pleasure so it would reside in the pleasure side of the Child mind [**any** source of pleasure would reside in this part of the Child.]. But for someone with painful experiences connected to sex, it can reside in the pleasure and pain part of the Child. In fact if the pain were severe enough then sex can reside totally in the pain part of the Child.

Where issues of morality, decency, social behaviour are drawn in, then sex can reside not only in the pleasure and pain side of the Child, but in the Parent as well. This is a disaster for a healthy sexual relationship, yet almost all adults in the UK have this complication to some degree [due mainly to social and cultural programming, these problems are not so severe in other countries.].

Sex in the Parent mind eventually leads to sexual dysfunction. Ranging from preferences: sadism/ masochism, to psychologically enforced abstinence: performance anxiety/ impotence/ vaginismus.

Due to the survival of the species we can "mate" in any of our three conscious minds. But it should be noted that this is an emergency capability and long term sexual problems can occur if the *wrong* mind is involved regularly.

Similarly a pleasurable experience for one person may be a painful experience for another. This makes global statements about Child activities very difficult: -

- Ice cream is a favourite amongst most people; therefore the consumption of ice cream is in the pleasure side of the Child.

Unless:- you have sensitive teeth, the last thing you saw your mother eat before she died of a heart attack was ice-cream, as a young child you were *bribed* with an ice-cream then abused, etc. Any of these would ensure that Ice cream was definitely **not** on the pleasure side of the Child.

- People like to eat spicy food, spend lots of money, go socialising, drink alcohol, etc.

Whatever you put on this list somebody, somewhere will have had an unpleasant experience with it, or have social/ moral/ religious/ etc. reasons against it. As such it will not be on the pleasure side [or it will be in both].

This leads to a lot of *vague* statements, using words like usually/ often/ normally/ almost/ generally. It is not that we do not know, but that there will usually be an exception to the rule.

Also I cannot write a book giving you information/ details that you can use to identify different Minds, Scripts, Frames of Reference, Stamp Collecting, etc. Unless I can give them as *hard rules*. So as you continue to read this book please think of *on average* or *in general* or *usual/ ly* etc.

If *you* know of an exception that **doesn't** mean the rule is invalid.

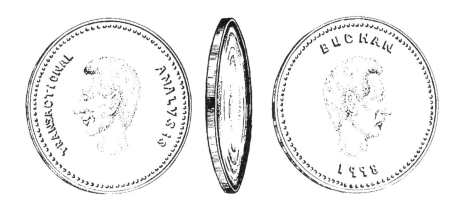

"In a healthy Child mind the "coin" would be on its edge. This is a neutral position being neither heads or tails. If the Child is becoming involved in something pleasurable then it will "fall" pleasure [tails] side up. If the Child is becoming involved in something potentially painful then it will "fall" pain [heads] side up."

This is a "birds eye view" of the coins. Demonstrating that once the coin "falls" face up it can only show the characteristics of that part of the Child until it is moved.

The Child mind like the coin appears to be different depending on which side you look at it. If it helps think of a positive/ pleasure aware Child and a negative/ pain aware Child as two separate identities. Since the pleasure side has completely different attitudes and behaviour from the pain side.

Pleasure: "I want" attitude, attracted to certain people, desires (sex, objects, people, food, clothing, fun, etc.), play now/ pay later, wants everything **now**, increasingly unable to recognise moral/ social/ religious/ ethical rules the deeper you sink into the Child mind.
 [The deeper you react the more overwhelming the mammalian response/ desires. This is true for pain and pleasure in the Child mind, and for the needs of the Parent mind.]

Pain: "Why me?" attitude, waiting to be "rescued", fearful of certain people, need to get away/ escape (suicide may be considered by the negative Child as a suitable method of escape!), anxiousness/ fearfulness/ worrying, overwhelmed by "what ifs?" and obsessive/ addictive behaviour the deeper you sink into the negative Child mind.

THE PARENT

The Child mind is used to measure our personal survival abilities at any given point and to offer optimum/ preferred routes to that survival. Hence our choice of food, clothes, jewellery, partner, fun, etc.

The Parent is used measure our ability to survive as a member of our **species**. Our parents survived long enough to have offspring, if we observe and then mimic our parent **we** will survive long enough to have offspring. As there are many poisonous and aggressive creatures in our world, the slightest deviation from our parents actions/ behaviour/ attitudes/ etc. could be lethal. Our unconscious mind truly believes that we may die or be injured if we fail to mimic our parents, when we become adults ourselves. So we often stick rigidly to black or white interpretations of our reality, in our Parent mind.

In our first few years of life the Parent mind develops as the sister/ brother of the Child. There is considerable debate as to whether the Parent at this stage is a true mind in its own right or merely part of the Child. It is generally agreed that eventually the Parent separates and does become a mind in its own right.

The Parent is created in our first few years of life by observing externally; this is usually the observation of our true parents and Other Significant Adults (OSAs). This includes relatives, teachers, religious leaders and any other adult that we may see regularly (this includes television presenters, cartoon characters, television puppets, etc.).

It should be noted that what we believe we perceive is quite different from reality, but no analytical skills are available that could allow us to recognise that these direct observations are misperceptions. An obvious example is the size difference between a baby and its mother. The daily observations in this situation would demonstrate to the child's Parent mind that *mothers* are huge, powerful and physically aggressive. That their mother has an opinion on everything and is prepared to enforce that opinion with verbal/ physical aggression and/ or deprivation.

Most of this misperception is purely caused by the significant difference in size between a mother and her baby. And has nothing to do with the mother's true intent. In fact, the more the mother loves and physically cares for her child, the more likely the physical differences will lend the child's Parent mind to believe that the mother is physically powerful and aggressive.

Even changing a nappy is a very physical event as perceived by the young baby. Many new misperceptions as to the aggressiveness of the mother are created with this type of every day event. Should the child no longer wish to wear the nappy; during the nappy change, the mother may hold the baby down with one hand (usually across the chest) whilst changing the nappy with the other hand. The more the baby wriggles around the more pressure the mother is likely to put on the baby's chest. In addition quite inadvertently, as the mother's attention focuses on nappies – talcum powder – baby wipes – safety pins etc. she may transfer her body weight to the hand holding down the baby while she reaches for any one of the above. This is likely to be a terrifying event for the young baby.

This may be easier for you to understand if you attempt to imagine that you are about to be cared for and changed by a 50ft tall creature weighing 3,500lbs. Said creature grasps you firmly around the chest and yanks you quite sharply from ground level to its eye level, then swings you quite quickly back to the ground. It then pins you to the ground with a hand that covers your entire rib area and starts to lean its entire 3,500lbs weight on to your chest.

Now imagine that you have no way of communicating to this creature of how you feel. You cannot explain that your ribs are beginning to, or are feeling as if they are about to, crack. You feel you cannot breathe. You attempt to wriggle or move away from the creature's hand only for it to place even more pressure on your chest.

Perhaps you are now getting an image of how it feels for a baby to have its nappy changed. Assuming this is a true image of the young child's impression of having its nappy changed, it would be perfectly reasonable to suggest that from a child's point of view, it has had an act of violence carried out against it by its mother and/ or father at least once every single day of its life. (*This is just one of the many pieces of evidence the Child will use to identify whether it is loved or unloved*).

As I will point out many times throughout this book, it is clearly not the intent of loving parents to cause pain and suffering to their babies. It is just a sad fact of life that however we care for our children, these misperceptions will occur.

It is a fact of human nature that a baby cannot care for itself; in fact, a human baby cannot even pull up a cover to keep warm let alone feed or change itself. As such, it is the responsibility of the adults connected to the child to feed and change it. And until an alternative form of care can be provided for babies, these misperceptions will continue to be perpetuated.

It is the intent of both TA and this book to allow adults to recognise that they themselves are the victims of these misperceptions. By using one's Adult mind, one can override these early misperceptions. It is not the intent of TA or this book to establish new models of baby care, as the ramifications of any changes in baby care usually require several generations before they become apparent. Until these processes can be investigated thoroughly, it is safer to accept the effects of our present method of child rearing and come to terms with these.

Because we observe our parents getting on with things, carrying out tasks and generally being involved with the necessities of life, we adopt task oriented processes within our own Parent mind. To put this simply, our Parent mind is essential for every day life because it just gets on with whatever task is at hand. It is unconcerned with the niceties of life and therefore is <u>unaware</u> of any feelings that may be connected to such tasks, or any grey area that may indicate such a task is unnecessary. It just does. As long as we remain in our Parent mind throughout any task that is required, we will carry out that task without any feeling.

However, carrying out perceived "Parental tasks" in our Child mind will rapidly build up all sorts of feelings, usually culminating in some way to resentment. It should therefore be obvious that *tasks* connected to our basic needs are best carried out by the Parent mind i.e. housework, shopping, etc.

It should be noted at this point that one of the purposes of this book is to allow the individual to gain a healthy balance of Minds; rather than suggesting that one mind is more important than another is.

The Parent mind is the home of our moral, religious, social and ethical frameworks; for life. The Parent mind accepts these frameworks and the rules within these frameworks, as black or white. There are no grey areas. Grey areas require thought to ascertain what actions or functions are appropriate that would not be appropriate when something is obviously black or white. This will prevent the Parent from getting on with the task in hand. (Such grey areas are usually the domain of the Adult mind). Occasionally, there appear to be conflicts when we observe other people's Parent minds i.e. a friend may choose to change their religion from Christianity to Judaism or Islam. This may seem a dramatic change of religious belief, but in the framework many things are similar: -

These particular religious beliefs, hold to one God/ distinct places of worship/ ceremony/ religious rules/ a book of instructions, history and prophecy/ commitment/ Prophets/ etc.

Considering this in the Parent mind then provided the rules have the same pattern, the individual has not actually changed religion but merely changed the title of that religion.

The Parent mind adopts the **fight** side of "fight flight".

In effect the Parent mind is initially competitive and pleasantly excited by the challenge, but can easily deteriorate into naked aggression if the stressor is unresolved. In the common understanding of stress the Parent mind would be recognised as positive stress. Where [well intentioned but inept] counsellors/ therapists suggest that we all need stress in our lives; it is positive/ Parental stress that they are usually referring to.

[It should be noted that the physical damage that occurs to the body during periods of stress occurs throughout positive stress as well as dis – STRESS. As such, some compensatory period should <u>always</u> be connected to positive stress prior to such global advice that we all need stress in our lives. During periods of meditation or hypnotic states, the immune system works more efficiently and the body repairs itself at a much higher rate. Thereby compensating for excessive demands on the body and mind. Therefore periods of <u>any</u> type of stress should be accompanied as soon as possible by a period of relaxation such as one would experience in hypnosis or meditation].

NB Road rage is identified in the same part of the unconscious Parent as the competitive enjoyment we find in sport (positive stress). I can hardly believe that stress counsellors are recommending that we all go out and enjoy road rage as a beneficial part of our development. [Any extreme anger or rage is found in the same part of the Parent as competitiveness. Again, I hope stress counsellors are **not** really suggesting that we **need** to reach a state where we could maim or kill, to ensure a healthy stress level?]

Quite often through social programming, the Parent is prevented from adopting a Fight response. This leads to build up of anxiety and depression in the Child mind. The social situation dictated that a Parental reaction is unacceptable, therefore a shift from the unconscious Parent to the unconscious Child occurs.

I.e. At a high-level award ceremony you are slandered by one of the award winners. The occasion and their new status as a hero/ ine prevents you from responding in your Parent even though you may have reacted in your Parent. At some point in this ceremony you may move into your unconscious Child and begin to anxiete/ symptom. It is the *social situation* that dictates much of (but not all!) the Parent response/ reaction.

[Note: In a different social climate you may remain in your Parent. e.g. in an archetypal "red neck" or "biker" bar; you hear the same slanderous comments. You may become verbally abusive [this often leads to a exchange of crude/ bawdy insults, the humour in this can "clear the air" and is probably the closest to an ideal solution!] or even start a fight.

NB. In the first situation, you are likely to store negative emotional charges leading to resentment/ anger causing you to take alternative action [perhaps litigation]. In the second situation provided you feel you won; both you and your opponent may feel justice has been met, the emotional charge has been released and everyone/ thing can get back to normal. Although the "Biker" route provided it doesn't become too physical is mentally healthier; sadly perhaps due to greed, moral/ social degeneracy and a lot of unscrupulous lawyers, many people seem to prefer the litigation route.]

Occasionally, there is a very dramatic shift from the unconscious Child (in the Flight response) to the unconscious Parent (in the Fight response). An example of this is a weaker animal that is cornered having run as far as it can, suddenly turning on the stronger animal in a very aggressive and dramatic way.

The Child and Parent minds use a different form of logic to that which we are used to in our rational thought processes. So even though the animal's position may appear hopeless, it may still win against all the odds by attacking/ surprising its aggressor.

A little extreme perhaps, but here is our "cornered" rabbit about to adopt the *Fight* response with a bear.

(Did I mention that having given some pretty vague *briefs* on each picture, I only gave Frank a couple of weeks to produce these illustrations?

"How am I supposed to draw a bear being fought off by a rabbit?" says Frank. "Give it a black *eye*" said I jokingly; "OK, then how do I draw an aggressive rabbit" he replied; "give it big teeth, you know a kind of primeval sabre toothed rabbit" I retorted flippantly.

Yes very funny Frank, now can I have the real picture!)

A more common example of this is the archetypal image of a small slightly built mother becoming exceptionally aggressive and violence in an attempt to protect her children.   Whatever actions her aggressor/ s may have carried out against her previously, being accepted without defence whilst they are directed towards herself.   Suddenly and dramatically are no longer acceptable because of the need to protect the infants.

She may be verbally abused or physically abused, putting up with it by withdrawing inwardly and/ or crying. Yet the moment her abusers turn to her child/ ren she [becoming instantly Parental] may turn into a snarling vicious animal.

In fact a family pet such as a docile and until this point very gentle/ affectionate dog may respond quite differently whilst caring for it's puppies:-

We have moved away from a modern understanding of TA. TA suggests that emotions are the domain of the Child mind [and occasionally the Adult]. Because of this, modern research into TA has ground to a halt because certain actions and behaviour cannot reasonably be explained if certain inappropriate emotion is in the Child. However, by accepting that certain types of emotion are purely Parental allows new areas to be researched or discovered in connection to human behaviour through TA. Whilst TA and this book are very much based on clinical work, they also rely heavily on common sense.

It is common sense to consider that the naked aggression of a powerful adult creature is far superior to the fear of a child in a life or death situation. Surely it is reasonable to accept that when the developing Parent mind is observing other significant adults and its parents, it will adopt the misperceived hugeness, aggressiveness and strength of the adult creatures around it.

The chemicals involved are adrenaline and nor-adrenaline. Usually people misunderstand the significance of an adrenaline release.

Adrenaline is a very powerful and <u>unpleasant</u> chemical.

Whilst both adrenaline and nor-adrenaline create similar physical changes: - shallow breathing, raised heartbeat, high blood pressure, certain muscles become tense etc. the psychological/emotional responses are quite different. Adrenaline causes feelings of low self-esteem, lack of confidence, feeling unable to cope, heightened sense of awareness, heightened self-awareness, anxiety and fear amongst others.

Powerful and positive feelings such as self-confidence, competitiveness, feeling in control etc. are created by a nor-adrenaline release. It should be noted that nor-adrenaline and adrenaline are released simultaneously and it is the amount that is predominant that dictates the emotional/ psychological state.

You may have realised that a predominant nor-adrenaline release pushes the individual into the fight response (Parental) whilst the predominant adrenaline release leads to the flight response (Child). This is the reason why <u>any</u> mammal can change instantly from the flight response to the fight or from the fight response to flight. It is merely the amount of chemical that is released that dictates the condition.

However, most mammals adopt habitual responses and whilst they can change, it is fairly rare. We would not therefore expect to be violently savaged by a rabbit, nor would we expect an angry bear to run away.

I knew this illustration would come in handy!

One angry bear "running away" and one violent rabbit just about to "savage" the bear.

(The nice thing about being the author is you can write all sorts of "snotty" things about the illustrations [and the illustrator], after they are placed within the text. So when the rude/ self-opinionated/ pompous illustrator says "I don't care whether you like them or not, I'm not changing them!"; you can get your own back!)

Have you been learning? If so what mind do you think I was in, when I made the comments about the illustrator?
Frank was "self-opinionated" when responding to my criticism. What mind do you think Frank was in?

The Adult

The Adult mind begins to form at ten months of age through the use of words. However, the Adult mind does not become fully functioning until somewhere between five and seven years of age. One of the reasons for this is that the Adult mind is a mixture of the actual words we understand and the hidden meanings behind those words. Young children learn words literally whereas adults tend to use words conceptually. It therefore takes four to six years to develop an understanding of concepts.

The Adult mind is unique to humans. In fact, it may be that it is the Adult mind that makes us human*. It hardly takes a genius to realise that it is not our "opposing thumbs" or the fact that we walk upright that makes us human.

These popular myths can easily be debunked merely by watching a documentary on racoons or orang-utans. The amazing dexterity that racoons demonstrate clearly puts us to shame therefore if our opposing thumbs i.e. the fact that we can grip is what makes us human then racoons would rule the earth. In addition if it is the fact that we can walk upright then many creatures such as orang-utans would also share world dominance with our own species. As we don't normally see racoons, orang-utans, or any other mammal for that matter building high-rise apartments or driving trains or any other intensive human behaviour, it is quite obvious that something else is responsible for our particular uniqueness.

*Humans are characterised by the title Homo *sapiens sapiens,* the second use of *sapiens* to distinguish from H. *sapiens* a genus of human primate to which we are part of. The title was given to "intelligent/ modern man" Cro-Magnon man to identify the difference in skills between early/ archaic H.*sapiens* approximately 400,000 years BP (before present) and Cro-Magnon man 35,000 years BP. Cro-Magnon man was the first **anatomically** modern human. However the human beings of 10,000 years BP were dramatically different **psychologically** [assessed through evidenced behaviour and achievement] to Cro-Magnon man. As such, the title Homo *sapiens rationalis* or H. *sapiens rationalis* would be more appropriate for the "reasoning" human beings from this date. It is as if the Adult mind were stunted or not fully developed in early Cro-Magnon man, appearing almost miraculously and very noticeably 10,000 years BP.

Mud hut villages, cattle farming [for meat], pottery and the cultivation of root crops during the next millennia, continuing to the domestication of sheep and cattle. Over the following two millennia: - copper and lead smelting, cattle also used for ploughing, irrigation, use of animals for milk, domestication of horses, maize and rice cultivation, etc. These are **enormous** advances in a relatively short period of time, requiring considerable reasoning abilities, the obvious domain of the **Adult mind**!

The Child and Parent minds are common to all mammals. However, the Adult is peculiar to human beings. It is therefore not an unreasonable premise to suggest that it is the Adult mind that makes us unique. Before I give you the characteristics of the Adult, you may be fascinated to know that we may not have evolved the Adult mind. Whether it is a God given gift or an accident of evolution is for you to decide. But any psychologist would recognise immediately that it is unlikely that we evolved our Adult mind. The facts are incredibly simple. With every other creature that has evolved a survival trait and/ or has evolved to fit a niche of nature, they always adopt that trait under pressure. In fact regardless or whether they are under pressure or not, most creatures will use their unique trait first.

Common sense will demonstrate this quite nicely. Imagine for a moment that you are unarmed and you have been cornered by a tiger (600lbs of claw, muscle and teeth), you will be stunned if the tiger attempted to reason with you rather than actually attacked you. The tiger will go through several recognisable processes prior to the final assault. Only when the tiger is convinced that the attack will be successful and/ or that you are unable to suitably defend yourself will it pounce. This procedure makes tigers and most other mammals relatively easy to capture since they will all go through set procedures at any stage in their natural fight or flight response.

This demonstrates quite clearly that any creature but in particular mammals will always use their natural/ evolved skills and instincts under pressure. No matter what behaviour they may have demonstrated beforehand and often no matter what training we may have given them, mammals will eventually revert to instinctive/ evolved behaviour under stress. The first mind we switch off under any form of pressure or stress is our <u>Adult</u> reverting to the Parent (fight) or the Child (flight).

Additionally, the Adult mind only appears to have been available in the form you would recognise now for approximately 8,000 to 10,000 years. In terms of evolution this is a ridiculously short time. Also homo erectus/ homo sapiens have been around for approximately 450,000 years so why didn't we have cities, automobiles, aircraft, computers etc. 400,000 years ago?

The Adult mind has three characteristics that again appear unique to human beings, these being the awareness of the passage of time, conceptual language and self- awareness to the degree we can have a conversation with ourselves mentally.

The Awareness of the Passage of Time

I would like you to think back for a moment about your first day at school. Can you remember how you got there? Can you remember what you did? Can you remember how old you were? Do you know how long it is since that first day at school?

The last question, is a trick question that demonstrates the awareness of the passage of time quite nicely. Most of us are well aware of how long it has been since we were involved in certain experiences. These may have been daily activities, weekly activities, monthly activities, yearly or even decades since certain things have happened to us. We understand these things. We actually talk in these terms pointing out how long it was and/ or how long it will be and in this peculiar way we can project our conscious awareness into the past or the future. Often talking about how long to our next vacation or what we might be doing on the weekend etc.

Other mammals do not appear to have this ability.

We use this awareness to facilitate and assist our modern lives. Many people ensure that their lives are not too cluttered by arranging appointments/ dates where specific times are given for certain activities. We even do this on a daily basis recognising that it may be two hours until lunch, and that lunch-time itself may consist of 30 minutes to 1 hour. After lunch, we recognise how many hours we have left to complete our work. We may schedule dental appointments, hairdressing appointments etc. - all given specific times and dates. We take all of this for granted since we have taught our Adult mind since early childhood to adopt this mechanism.

For those academics that may wish to argue with this premise I am clearly not discussing diurnal variation or seasonal recognition. Even the most basic creatures can recognise the difference between light and dark. More sophisticated creatures can recognise the difference between summer and winter, but other than cartoons, one would hardly expect two lizards talking about what a wonderful summer they had last year and what activities they intend to get up to this coming summer.

One of the side effects of the awareness of the passage of time is heightened anxiety and/ or frustration. We now have new threats to our well being merely by being aware of the passage of time. Deadlines, traffic jams, missed appointment, impending appointments etc. all cause consternation and pressure. Continued on the next page.
Additional frustration and/ or anxiety can be caused through shared activity with young children who of course have not developed their Adult mind and therefore have no understanding of the passage of time.

We have all had experiences of young children on car journeys where having just pulled away from the kerb on perhaps a 100 mile journey. The young child in the back says, "are we there yet?" Regardless of the reassurances of the distance to be travelled (in time i.e. 2 to 3 hours) the child will regularly ask, "are we there yet" or "are we nearly there yet?"

Also we may have given a child permission to play with other children on the condition that they come back at certain time intervals i.e. 15 minutes, 30 minutes or an hour. On realising that the particular time interval that we give our child has long passed, we may become very anxious or distressed totally unaware that the child in question has no way of understanding or recognising that that time has gone by.

Even where the child has been given a watch, with **strict** instructions that when the big hand and little hand reach certain positions, they are to return home without fail; the child does not have an internal mechanism that would allow them to understand that sufficient time has gone by to **look** at the watch in the first place.

We as adults rarely recognise that young children are not human and therefore require the additional care that a non-human mammal in human society would require. No horse trainer would dream of abandoning their horse in Central Park with strict instructions to meet them again at a certain time and place. This is incredibly obvious whether it is a dog, a cat, a rabbit or the horse in question, we accept quite happily that none of these creatures are capable of understanding the time limits in question.

Yet any mammal that has been trained **does** recognise human language otherwise how could they follow that training? Most people will accept this, yet for some odd reason, still expect their two and a half or three year old child to understand time limits, perhaps arguing that the child understands human language. What we fail to recognise is that like any other creature (excluding adult humans) that uses language, young children use literal language rather than conceptual language.

<u>Conceptual Language</u>

It is easier to begin explaining conceptual language by identifying literal language. Other creatures including young human beings use literal language. In the context of this book, literal language is used to describe any language where each individual word either has one dedicated meaning or is used as a proper noun i.e. a title. If I asked a young child (2½ to 3 years) to point to the door they would usually be capable of doing this. If I then asked them if they *knew* what it was, they would probably reply "door".

I as an adult would then mistakenly believe that the child knew what a door is. This couldn't be further from the truth. To a young child using only their Parent or Child mind, a door is just an ornate part of the wall. The fact that it swings backwards and forwards is neither here nor there. This is because in literal language *door* is the title given to that particular ornate part of the wall. There are no other facts or concepts given to the word door.

However, in conceptual language (the medium of the Adult mind), there are hundreds of thousands of facts hidden behind the word door: -
Materials: woods (thousands of species), glass, PVC, metal, etc.
Combinations: materials almost unlimited, paints, colours schemes, almost unlimited.
Finishes: paints (gloss, eggshell, vinyl etc.), varnish, wax, oil, natural, etc.

Types: Interior doors, exterior doors, vehicle, household appliance, cupboard, etc.

Furniture: (This being door furniture rather than household furniture) knobs, handles, hinges, letter boxes, etc. Again styles and types almost unlimited.

Access: hinged (normally left or right sided but many examples of doors hinged at the top or bottom i.e. hatchback, cat flap, dishwasher etc.), revolving, concertina, roller, "up and over", and automatic (i.e. sliding doors). The latter five are mechanisms that allow a door to open without any form of hinge. However, the actual door in each of these cases can be made of similar materials to a conventional door (i.e. hinged).

When we are using our Adult mind we access hundreds of thousands of facts prior to using any every day object that we may come across, the door being a simple example. If I wish to go to extremes, there are millions perhaps even billions of combinations of different colours, materials, furniture and types of access for doors.

Technically, there are more facts in connection to the concept of doors than we actually have storage area for them in the physical brain. Perhaps this is something for academics to worry about; we can just enjoy this astonishing idea that our Adult mind has such a phenomenal amount of information available about the things that we come across. This is conceptual language.

Conceptual language in the meaning of this book involves the idea of thinking and corresponding (talking, writing, images etc.) in concepts where each word used has a phenomenal reservoir of hidden information.

We regularly give a literal instruction that has a conceptual direction. On a lighter note this can be used in a fun manner where ambiguous comments are handed back to us with the literal intent. Unfortunately, conceptual instructions can cause serious distress and harm to the emotional and psychological development of young children trying to cope in an Adult/ conceptual environment with a literal understanding of the world.

However, using literal language gives a young child (i.e. 3 to 4) a tremendous advantage in learning a second or third language since they only have to learn and remember one meaning/ fact/ title for each word.

Whereas adults may have an unconscious block, since they are well aware that every word they come across has thousands, tens of thousands and even hundreds of thousands of pieces, of hidden information. All of which has to be learned in the new language otherwise we are required to think in our mother tongue then translate to the new language. Whilst a young child that stores words in a literal understanding within their Child or Parent minds can actually think *in either language having only one meaning/ fact/ title to consider at any one time.*

The Child and Parent minds tend to *think* in images, feelings and simple words. Information is therefore accepted and passed simply and accurately. However, the disadvantage is that there are rarely "grey" areas. To the unconscious Child or Parent things are either right or wrong, good or bad, liked or disliked; this leads to "either/ or" type thinking i.e. if this is right, then that must be wrong.

In an Adult world this is at best misleading and at worst life-threatening.

A simple example is people who are ill (therefore more likely to be in their Child or Parent mind [usually the Child]) may give up their conventional medicine in the mistaken belief that a complementary medicine will work instead. The Adult understanding of "complementary medicine" is that it is complementary to; rather than an alternative to, any other form of medicine therefore should have been used in conjunction with conventional treatment. But the Child mind's view is often that if the complementary medicine works the conventional medicine doesn't. i.e. a cancer sufferer undergoing conventional (but perhaps very unpleasant) treatment may abandon it in the belief that a change of diet, regular aromatherapy sessions and a course of positive thinking will cure them instead.

As a practitioner of complementary medicine, I would be horrified to think that someone mistakenly believed that they didn't require any conventional care in a life-threatening situation merely because they received counselling or hypnotherapy. NB An exception to this is alternative medicine where the obvious suggestion is that it is an alternative route to recovery.

It is my personal opinion that alternative therapy is often an ego boosting exercise on behalf of the practitioner and their therapy; since provided the client improves to the level that they require, does it really matter to the client if they used additional things to speed up their improvement?

There is no doubt amongst hypnotherapists that hypnosis can be used to speed the recovery rate after any form of trauma, in particular direct physical damage to the body. The recovery rate from operations can be dramatically enhanced through the use of hypnosis and appropriate suggestions. However, should any of those hypnotherapists (including myself) suffer a firearms wound or a broken leg, we would hardly run a hypnotic procedure and expect full recovery without any type of conventional assistance.

Therefore the either/ or response from the Child mind in these situations is actually a threat to its own survival. This alone is a perfect example of the difficulties a child faces when corresponding with adults.

Self Awareness

There are many different types of and/ or degrees of self-awareness and it is quite clear that many mammals are self-aware.
But there is an intensity of self-awareness within the Adult mind that is quite unique.

For example, a dog is quite capable of independent action and thought. The dog may observe birds in the garden after a period of time the dog may chase them off and dig up a buried bone. Whether the dog genuinely believed the birds were going to eat its bone or not, it is quite clear that the dog in some way was thinking to itself. This is the basic form of self-awareness. In a more obvious example the dog becomes hungry and scratches at its food cupboard or carries its food bowl to its master, clearly some form of thought and awareness is involved.

However, the level of self-awareness in the Adult mind is far beyond the basic recognition that one is hungry and that the solution involves an action.

In the Adult mind the self-awareness is taken to the degree where we can have a conversation with ourselves mentally. We can discuss issues; ideas or even ponder thoughts all without saying a word. Ideally, the skill can be used to observe, monitor and even affect the Child and Parent minds although unless this is pointed out most people are unaware of this ability.

It should be noted at this point that only the upper portion of the "iceberg" can be accessed therefore in a relaxed state, a larger portion of the conscious Child/ Parent can be accessed and affected, perhaps even reprogrammed. Conversely a stressful situation or lack or strokes leading to the iceberg sinking reduces the amount of access the Adult has until we are purely reacting animals surviving on a fight or flight response alone. Obviously there are many different levels that the Adult mind can **access** a Child or Parent and it should also be noted that the ability to access the Child or Parent does not guarantee an ability to **affect** the Child or Parent. The same rules, however, apply in that, during a relaxed state the likelihood of an ability to affect the Child or Parent is increased.

The Adult mind is primarily a conscious mind where self-awareness is one of the primary skills. However, the access to conceptual information becomes a habit and therefore appears unconscious but in the early stages of development it is quite obvious that we constantly consciously review certain facts and information before making our decisions.

An understanding of mathematics is a good example.

A young child (5 years) may constantly have to refer consciously to addition and subtraction and multiplication whilst working with small numbers.
This would make even simple algebra impossible since there is a limit to how much information we can deal with in the conscious mind at any one time. However, once the ability to make simple additions, subtractions and multiplication's; become habits; then algebra becomes a much easier subject to work with.

I.e. $Y = 4 \times 3 - 7$, you as an Adult can work this out in your head probably quite quickly. A child that hasn't developed multiplication and subtraction as a habit may find that the Adult mind keeps closing down, as it does not have the skills and knowledge to even understand the mathematical requirements. Their initial response may be to write each calculation down i.e. $4 \times 3 = 3$

$$\begin{array}{r} 3 \\ 3 \\ \underline{3} \\ 12 \end{array}$$ then $12 - 7 = 5$

MAMMALIAN MINDS

There has been regular reference to *mammalian* minds as if they are something different or extra. Our mammalian minds are part of our human heritage. Often we *are* our mammalian minds in the way we react and behave! So much so that at one point in this chapter, young children were referred to as "not human and therefore require the additional care that a non-human animal in human society would require."

It is important to point out again, that we are mammals first and humans second. It is the **Adult** mind that brings/ gives us our human nature.

In a young child the Adult is insufficiently developed to be used properly.

Whilst there are vestiges of the Adult from about 30 months onwards, it is a rare and gifted child that has a fully functioning Adult prior to four and a half years of age.
Sadly there are many <u>adults</u> that do not evidence a fully functioning Adult!

It is the mammal in us all that creates the greatest problems and threats to human society. If this is ignored then the potential benefits you may gain from this book will be lost.

Every mammal requires a system/ program/ mind/ etc. that can allow it to survive at its optimum pace. Each mammal needs a process where they can eat, sleep, play, rest and procreate safely. Mammals also require social skills, regardless of whether they are pack/ herd animals or lone hunters.

The **Child** and **Parent** minds as our **mammalian minds** provide all of this and more.

By direct observation/ experience linked to pain/ pleasure the Child mind in any mammal can offer the optimum pace for survival.

By direct observation and mimicking the Parent mind in any mammal can offer social skills and other rules of conduct.

Processes for eating, sleeping, playing, resting and procreating are shared between the Child and Parent minds. All of these processes are carried out at a comfortable level unless a threat to survival [or food if the mammal is a hunter] is identified. At which point the Child will react in the Flight mode of stress, whilst the Parent will react in the Fight mode. All behaviour at this point is governed by these instinctive reactions. However each species has its evolved preference: -

A rabbit is more likely to adopt a Child reaction, reacting in the Flight response and running away.

A rhinoceros is more likely to adopt a Parental reaction, reacting in the Fight response and charging head-on.
A domestic cat may begin Child, choosing a Flight reaction until cornered, at which point it may become Parental, reacting in the Fight response.

All of the requirements of a mammal's life are recorded/ encoded within the Child and Parent minds. To assist in meeting these requirements mammals are *driven* chemically, hormonally and with minute electrical charges. *Driven* to eat, sleep, play, rest and mate. In some cases *driven* to hoard things, usually but not always food. *Driven* to gain the highest status in their particular pack/ herd/ etc.

There are no long drawn out reasoning processes involved with these minds: -

1. Something is either a threat or it isn't.

2. Something is either food or it isn't.

3. Something is either a mate or it isn't.

4. Something is either higher in the pack/ herd/ etc. or it isn't.

5. Something is either needed or it isn't.
There is no middle ground; there is no requirement for reasoning or higher conscious thought.

Life under these terms is simple. Decisions are almost made for you: -

1. If it's a threat, react in the appropriate mind.

2. If it's food, eat it [or catch it and eat it].

3. If it's a mate, court it.

4. If it's higher in the pack/ herd/ etc. behave accordingly.

5. If you need it, get it!

Most issues are basic, generally black or white. There is a tendency to adopt an "either/ or" attitude, either this is right or that is right. It is rare that a mammalian mind can accept both as right or both as wrong.
We usually accept these things quite happily for **other** mammals, yet become uncomfortable/ disturbed when applying these things to ourselves.

This is unfortunate, since many so called *Justice* systems ignore these issues. Juveniles become punished for behaving normally under the circumstances they feel they are in. Even adults are punished for certain types of mammalian behaviour.

A fair/ humane system would address these issues, using a different educational process, self-responsibility and a "consequences" process rather than a punishment regime.

Our younger children, because they are not yet Adult, can **only** respond in the above ways, they only have their Child and Parent minds to guide them.

If we wish them to be more human then a careful change to their upbringing will encourage faster development of the Adult mind.

If we wish them to have less "hang-ups", then caring for them with an understanding of **their** mammalian view of the world is important.

That our children need *upbringing, care, understanding,* etc. that takes into account their mammalian nature, if they are to grow into healthy adults.

Finally it is important to recognise the Child and Parent minds as mammalian rather than human, since the mammalian *drives* in these minds can over-ride the Adult human mind under certain circumstances [usually connected to eating, sleeping, playing, resting, sex, power and money (power and money represent pack status!)].

*Whether we like it or not, human beings are still a mixture of mammal [Child and Parent] and reason [Adult]. Under sufficient pressure we revert to mammal, at which point we are **driven** to meet mammalian needs.*

Fight or Flight: The Child [shown literally] adopts the Flight response, whereas the Parent [cue caveman] adopts the Fight response. These are primeval/ mammalian responses; there is no rational thought involved!
(NB Frank's been up to his sneaky tricks again, how real is the tiger? Sometimes we adopt a fight or flight response to our perceptions rather than reality!)

PERTINENT POINTS to PONDER (PPP's)

- There are **three** minds: - the **Parent**, **Adult** and **Child**.

JOINT ISSUES

- The Parent and Child are common to all mammals, and are the minds we are born with.

- The Parent and Child resemble icebergs in that the majority of each is unconscious, with a constantly moving section available to our conscious awareness.

- If we react in our Parent or Child it is assumed that the small conscious portion has or soon will, sink completely into the unconscious mind.

- When reacting in the Parent the Fight side of stress is adopted, leading to aggression/ anger/ over control.

- When reacting in the Child the Flight side of stress is adopted, leading to anxiety/ fear/ panic.

CHILD

- The Child is created during the first few (approximately 0-5 yrs) years of life, by observing how we feel, against anything we may observe or experience.

- Whilst there are only two primary feelings in the Child, pain or pleasure, there is an almost limitless number of types and intensities that can be felt.

- The Child retains a young childlike self-perception and attitude; it is easier to think of the Child as permanently five to six years of age.

- We are our Child mind! Whenever you think of self and the things you like, want, are attracted to, etc. you are in the domain of the Child.

- For a brief period during puberty additional sources of pain and pleasure are recorded in the Child.

- Free pleasure and creativity are positive traits of the Child.

- Increase in social harmony/ happiness and artistic advances are the social/ cultural positive traits of the Child.

- Anxiety and irrational fear are negative traits of the Child.

- Stress, anxiety, depression, addictions and general dissatisfaction are the social/ cultural traits of the Child.

PARENT

- The Parent is created during the first few years of life by direct external observation of any significant person during that period. Unlike the Child, the Parent continues to grow provided the incoming data meets previously established guidelines.

- Whilst the primary feelings in the Parent are total self-confidence/ competitiveness and anger/ rage, it is rare that we are consciously aware at the time.

- The Parent retains a "middle-aged"/ judgmental attitude, it may be easier to think of the Parent as an exaggeration of our true parents.

- Our Parent mind is the total repertoire of opinions/ judgements/ conduct/ social, moral and religious rules/ etc. available for everyday use.

- "Doing things" without unnecessary thought and keeping to the rules are the positive traits of the Parent.

- Rage and judgmental behaviour are the negative traits of the Parent.

- War and punishment are the social/ cultural negative traits of the Parent.

- Mass achievement such as the enormous implementation of industrial and social structures during the Victorian era [Rail networks, Shipping routes, gas supplies, mains water, sewage, etc.] are the social/ cultural positive traits of the Parent. *

*Where a positive Parental culture hands over these achievements to a negative Parent or negative Child culture, as a general rule the physical structure will deteriorate. I.e. Rail services will collapse, shipping will reduce, vast areas will lose or fail to receive basic water supplies, etc. Usually the deeper the negativity the greater the collapse.

ADULT

- The Adult is created from approximately 10 months of age and can be added to throughout life. However the Adult is not fully functioning until approximately 5 years of age.

- Whilst the Adult may appear fascinated or absorbed it is unlikely that it has any true feelings. Feelings felt consciously are either through direct access of the Parent/ Child, or are "borrowed" from the Parent/ Child.

- The Adult has a perception of the passage of time, basically if you know how long it has been since? Or how long it will be till? You are using the Adult.

- The Adult is self aware to the degree that we can have a mental conscious conversation with our selves in our own mind. Whilst both the Parent and the Child "borrow" this facility it is primarily an Adult mind skill.

- The Adult mind uses conceptual language whilst both the Parent and Child prefer literal language. [There is an intermediary lexicon used by all three minds, but it is far too complicated to describe in a dozen chapters let alone one paragraph! Also it is only of interest to academics, since unlike **all** of the other issues in this book, the intermediary lexicon may be too complex to be easily modified.].

- The Adult mind is the primary difference between humans and other mammals.

- In stress the Adult is increasingly switched off, in direct proportion to the intensity of stress.

- In some people the Adult may be temporarily de-commissioned, causing them to rely totally on Child/ Parent perceptions and reactions.

- There is little if any evidence [at this time] that the Adult mind is a direct result of "Darwinian" evolution; it may be an accident/ by-product of evolution, or it may be a "gift of God".

- Evidence of the Adult mind [as it is used today] only goes back approximately 8,000 years BC. As such, Homo *sapiens sapiens* (Cro-Magnon man/ modern human) is a misnomer since a "new" ability to modify the environment and rapidly increasing complexities in social/ cultural behaviour occurred at this time. Perhaps a better term would be Homo *rationalis* or H. *sapiens rationalis*, to indicate this dramatic and relatively modern reasoning ability of the Adult.

Although not mentioned in the previous text, it is possible that birds and reptiles have genetic or pre-programmed Child and Parent responses.
Or that Parent/ Child processes are *imprinted* instantly, rather than through regular observation.

STROKES

The term Transactional Analysis gives the impression that some form of transaction is analysed. The currency of exchange within the transaction is referred to as a "Stroke". Strokes and/ or lack of Strokes, affect every aspect of Transactional Analysis. Stamp Collecting, Game Playing, Scripts, reactions in the Parent and Child, etc. all are aggravated by a lack of Strokes; as all are eased by a surplus of Strokes.

Strokes are the unconscious mind's measurement of our survival and existence.

Quite simply, if we do not have enough Strokes our unconscious mind thinks we are dying [**now**, rather than at some vague point in the future].

This may come from the original recognition/ use or creation of Strokes.

When we are born we haven't learned to focus our hearing or sight, in addition our rational/ conscious mind has not yet developed. However, we can recognise if we are touched. A human baby is particularly ill adapted to survive and relies totally on the adult creature for survival. A human baby cannot feed itself, and may even be too weak to pull up a cover to keep warm. Quite simply, if a baby is not being touched, it is not being fed and <u>will die</u>. Therefore at this stage these touches/ Strokes are essential for life.

In fact a baby receiving sufficient food but a lack of Strokes can develop *Marasmus,* a condition where the body "wastes away" or fails to develop fully.

It cannot be emphasised too many times that in early childhood, **a lack of Strokes results in** poor emotional/ mental/ physical development, then if severe **death!**

[It should also be noted that where poor emotional / mental development has occurred from lack of Strokes; a consistent surplus will often speed recovery, even reversing the condition.]

To put this as simply as possible: imagine you are leaving your house to go shopping or to work or whatever. As you open your front door you see a tiny kitten on the doorstep, you bend down and *stroke* the kitten. The kitten mews/ purrs or rubs its body against your legs. You have literally given the kitten a Stroke and by replying [regardless as to whether it was vocal or physical] the kitten has given you a Stroke.

Perhaps you are expecting the kitten; you leave a saucer of milk, although you may not see the kitten, you have in leaving the milk given it a Stroke. Even though the kitten may not drink the milk until several hours after you have left, an exchange of strokes has occurred.

Alternatively as you *stroke* the kitten it claws your hand drawing blood. An exchange of Strokes has still occurred: you gave the kitten a positive Stroke [sometimes referred to as a warm fuzzy (Claude Steiner, The Original Warm Fuzzy Tale, Jalmar Press.) because of the feeling it generates inside on receipt]. The kitten returned a negative Stroke [sometimes referred to as a cold prickly (Claude Steiner) because of the feeling it generates inside] by scratching you. After all, you very much know you're alive when something hurts; as much as you know you're alive when something feels good.

Since people want to feel warm and fuzzy rather than cold and prickly, some people give "plastic" Strokes. These are cold prickly Strokes that are offered as if they were warm fuzzy Strokes. Plastic Strokes sound right but leave bad feeling. Plastic Strokes require deviousness and are usually the domain of human beings rather than other mammals.

All Strokes are functional in that the unconscious mind uses any Stroke to evidence its survival and existence. Although for obvious reasons positive Strokes are more beneficial than negative/ plastic.

People get into habits of collecting and giving certain types of Stroke. If we have particularly low self-esteem we may only collect negative or plastic Strokes; mistakenly believing that's all that we deserve. Under these circumstances positive Strokes would be ignored or misperceived as plastic Strokes. "You look nice today" may be taken as sarcasm or may be taken as: - you don't normally look good, today must be an exception.

Sometimes we misperceive in childhood that positive Strokes are so rare or difficult to collect and that negative Strokes are more easily available. Under these circumstances we lazily only attempt to get negative Strokes when we grow up.
Even our work assessments often adopt this process where copious positive work is often ignored whilst one or two mistakes are highlighted leading to low assessments and resentment.

Relationships often follow a similar process where our humanness is ignored. i.e. All humans (not being machines) are fallible, yet many people [again suffering from meanness of spirit] will sue for divorce if their partner makes one mistake or shows one human failing. In fact one particularly sick form of this is in the idea of "treat them mean, keep them keen", where cruelty and meanness are supposed to be the foundation for a successful relationship. This perpetuates negative Stroking, building up resentment and unhappiness, which then spreads throughout society.

Positive Stroking creates generosity of spirit and kindness leading to happiness. When this spreads through society crime reduces, addictive behaviour reduces, good neighbourliness increases, people have more patience and understanding, basically things get better all around.

Sadly at present in western society negative/ plastic Stroking is encouraged. This is due in part to PC'ers and lawyers, since *social* Stroking through certain forms of Political Correctness is now *demanded*, thereby building resentment. Where some forms of positive Stroking can be misconstrued as patronising, and as such have been withdrawn socially. Otherwise litigation or the threat of litigation tends to follow fairly quickly if things are not proven to benefit the potentially aggrieved party.

Basically self-responsibility is being eroded; don't wait till someone offers you a stroke, don't wait till someone legislates for your particular minority group to be given Strokes through society; if you recognise that you need Strokes it is your responsibility to create them! Give Positive Strokes away freely and without thought of reward or return. Not only will you receive them back tenfold, you gain them constantly through your generosity of spirit.

Or sit back and wait, then Take! Take! Take! Everybody else is doing it why shouldn't you?
This is the attitude that has created the society that we live in today. A society filled with fear, resentment, greed, spitefulness, etc.

A society *you* live in!

Many mammals use Strokes to *evidence* that they exist and are existing to a certain standard. Strokes are peculiar to living creatures and are shared between species. As seen in the kitten example. Whilst cats are perfectly comfortable Stroking each other, they may happily accept a Stroke from a human.

However in rare circumstances Strokes may be given to and gained from inanimate objects.

There are a few people that are so affectionate towards their car/ motorbike that they not only name the machine they may openly Stroke it! In fact for some people polishing their car/ motorbike is a form of Stroking. This is a direct form of Stroking; for many people an indirect unconscious/ semi-conscious form of Stroking occurs when they *play* with or *stroke* a pen/ key ring/ etc. whilst **thinking** about someone else. They gain Strokes from the person they are thinking about even though that second person has no knowledge or idea that they are being thought about.

This brings up an important point! Gaining a Stroke from someone else even though they may not be directly involved doesn't mean that person has lost a Stroke. Where Strokes are given freely through care/ love/ compassion/ etc. the giver rarely loses any Strokes and often gains Strokes through such generosity. It's as if the person receiving the Stroke gains a full Stroke; whilst the person giving the Stroke also receives a half Stroke at the same time. For every Stroke we give to someone else provided that they need it, that we give freely without any thought of reward or return we gain something from it. Perhaps a partial Stroke or if the gesture is generous enough a full Stroke or even more!

*Free Strokes given with generosity of spirit return more than is given **even** if the Stroke is rejected.*

However where Strokes are demanded or stolen from someone there is almost always a Stroke loss; both for the recipient and for the person they are taken from. It's as if the person the Stroke is taken from loses a full Stroke; yet the person that demanded/ stole the Stroke only receives half a Stroke. Obviously if this type of behaviour is carried out in a relationship then it [the relationship] is ultimately doomed; unless fresh sources of Strokes can be found.

Strokes demanded or stolen, Strokes given because we should or ought to, Strokes given with bad grace usually cause resentment and meanness of spirit.

Although very young children often give and receive Strokes quite freely there comes a point where fear or resentment causes them to keep their Strokes to themselves. At this *Point of Commitment* they change becoming more self-centred and mean of spirit. This is a crucial moment as to whether this child will grow up to be a Stroke thief/ Game Player/ etc. and/ or whether they are sowing the seeds for suicide/ depression/ addictive behaviour/ anti-social behaviour/ etc. in their adult life.

As a general rule people who are free with their Strokes are gentle kind hearted and usually truly happy. People that are mean with their Strokes [or expect a return] are usually lacking in spirit often self-centred and rarely happy [often mistaking lack of unhappiness as happiness].

We can choose at any point in our lives which type of person we wish to be; provided we are genuine and consistent. However in western society we generally gravitate to meanness of spirit if we do nothing.

I am reminded of that oft used quote "all that is required for evil to flourish, is for good men to do nothing".

Meanness of spirit is a form of evil, since it affects both the originator and everyone around them.

At between four to seven years of age strokes go through a process of metamorphosis from physiological to psychological; from touch to **words!**

From this day onwards the childhood saying "sticks and stones may break my bones, but words will never hurt me" couldn't be further from the truth.   Words and even lack of words, plus gestures or lack of gestures can now have a devastating effect on the individual.   The primary cause of this is that Strokes even though they are now just words and/ or gestures still retain their original survival value.

Basically, regardless of whether they are physically tangible such as touch or psychological such as words, the unconscious mind genuinely believes that we are dying if we are low on Strokes.

Because of this Strokes are the "raison d'être" of Transactional Analysis.

Throughout this book you may misperceive that the Parent, Adult and Child/ Scripts/ Game Playing/ Stamp Collecting/ etc. stand-alone and can be analysed and changed in their own right. This is only partially true. Though they are traditionally presented this way to aid understanding.

Every one of these aspects of TA, is affected in some way by Strokes, whether it is a Stroke balance itself that aggravates the situation as in Scripts or the actual need to replenish the Stroke balance as in Game Playing.

[Although if the Stroke balance is positive then other aspects of TA can be accessed and reviewed individually.]

An understanding of any of the above issues will allow some improvement in any psychological condition and many physical conditions. They even allow changes to be made. However such improvement and changes may be easily lost by failing to maintain a good Stroke balance.

Whenever Strokes are considered, it is essential to remember that from the unconscious mind's point of view, a shortage is linked to the impression that death is imminent. Therefore an acute shortage of Strokes will usually lead to a fight or flight (mammalian response in the Parent or Child minds) response or unconsciousness/ paralysis (reptilian response).

[As in other aspects of TA there are three degrees in Stroke loss, or generation.]

First degree Stroke loss is a daily nuisance, where someone's behaviour or words may make you feel uncomfortable in some way. You feel comfortable and in control some of the time; yet other times you feel anxious and uncomfortable. You may cope perfectly well in one environment, such as work, yet out of control in another such as your relationship. Or suffer mixed feelings regardless of your activities. But these rarely get out of hand.

In second degree Stroke loss you will begin to feel so uncomfortable that you will have a driving need to verbally attack [Parent] or avoid [Child] the person/ activity/ source in question. Usually through social conduct, attack is unacceptable and you will gravitate toward the Child mind becoming more and more irrational in your dealings with the source.

During second degree Stroke loss stress symptoms will begin to surface, with regular Fight or Flight responses occurring.

As previously mentioned in PAC the iceberg begins to sink until unconscious/ instinctive Child mind reactions take over. Even to the point where psychosomatic illness may occur.

Classic work problems occur as you find your mouth saying "Yes, of course I can do more work/ work overtime/ cover for someone else/ etc."; as your mind is desperately thinking **No!** Or Why me? Can't someone else do it? What will I tell my wife/ husband/ partner?

You are far more likely to take time off work for a minor cold or sniffles, than you would in first degree Stroke loss. You are far more likely to suffer from a serious cold or influenza with second degree Stroke loss.

If the primary Stroke loss is in your relationship, then things can get pretty uncomfortable. Leading to more aggressive Game Playing, and/ or resentment through Stamp Collecting, and/ or a change in the Point of Commitment, etc. As this becomes chronic, a gradual deterioration into third degree, and therefore divorce or violence is likely. Using an intermediary such as Relate may **temporarily** alleviate the situation, but if Stroke loss continues then such measures are ultimately doomed.

This will deteriorate into third degree stroke loss when the iceberg becomes completely submerged.

In third degree stroke loss, your reaction may become so severe that physical illness occurs. Just the thought of meeting the person/ situation responsible for most of your Stroke loss, could make you physically ill.

As with any degree of stroke loss, anxiety and eventually depression are constant companions. The Child mind worries, anxietes and depresses; whilst attempting avoidance such as symptoms, obsessive behaviour, over eating, panic attacks, etc.

The intensity and pervasiveness of worry is directly connected to the degree of Stroke loss.

i.e. in first degree you may become slightly concerned and occasionally dwell on certain issues in your life.

In second degree, worry becomes repetitive and fixates on many issues in your life. The duration of worry brings on a pattern of conditions and symptoms.
The longer the period of worry in days, weeks, months, years the greater the deterioration in the individual. Therefore psychosomatic conditions will surface and gradually be added to or be replaced by physiological conditions. Obviously this will become third degree as the actual symptoms aggravate the Stroke loss. Depression, mental illness, suicide or death through actual physical failure of the organism will ensue.

Ultimately confirming that the unconscious belief that Strokes are a measurement of survival or actual existence is correct.

Whether or not the belief that loss of Strokes leads to death is the cause of death or the *actual loss* of strokes themselves lead to death is debatable.

The end result is the same either way.

Ultimately, whether real or imagined, third degree Stroke loss (unless interrupted) is terminal.

There are also three degrees of Stroke generation where first degree produces short bouts of cheerfulness and a general feeling of well being.

Second degree produces a sort of "Gung-ho" attitude where everything is wonderful and the feeling of well being becomes very intense leading to euphoria. In this state it can gradually lead to major changes in our "Frames of reference", even deteriorating into Manic behaviour.

Third degree produces "spiritual" experiences and ecstasy.

*As usual I would like to remind readers that the ideal is a balance, rather than suggesting that we should all pursue as many Strokes as possible. However the occasional third degree **generation** of Strokes, is much preferable to third degree loss!*
[Third degree Stroke generation produces similar effects to many "recreational" drugs without the side effects; plus of course its legal!]

*Stroke loss is an inevitable process of **modern** life.*

Every aspect of western culture has the potential to strip Strokes at a phenomenal rate. [Strokes were originally lost or gained in contact with other people. This was the traditional mechanism!]

In modern life Strokes are lost in every day situations such as: -

Sitting in traffic jams, without any contact with others.

Being late: - for work, for a meeting, for a partner, with a task, etc. all strip Strokes rapidly and without concern for age, sex, social status, race, etc.

Failing to attain targets.

Not matching media images of body, face, clothes, social standing, etc.

Getting old, being too young, passing 30/ 40/ 50/ 60 years of age.

Having the wrong partner, not having a partner, having children, not having children.

Renting a house, buying a house, having a house that is too big or too small, having a house in the wrong neighbourhood, having a house in the right neighbourhood but the wrong size/ type, etc.

The list is endless.

There are good ways of generating Strokes and poor ways.

Good ways to generate Strokes include intimacy where a safe environment is created to share personal ideas and feelings. Receiving physical attention such as a massage or aromatherapy are also good ways to increase your Stroke balance.

Past-timing [a TA term] involving shared bitching/ gossiping/ complaining about whatever? Or enthusiasm for a shared hobby or interest. However the conversation almost always covers the same ground, using the same words and phrases. It's almost as if you know before you start what you are going to say!
Bitching could be about the world, world affairs, a specific political party, or a specific politician. "The trouble with the world is....", "If it wasn't for the Communists.....", "If I was President...", "Used to be a time when....", etc.

Interests can be anything: -

"You know Harley Davidsons' used to be **real** bikes before they started putting in suspension/ rubber engine mounts/ electric starters/ etc.", "Yeah, I remember the Pan head, now there was an engine!" "Yup!"

"See the Presidents been at it again", "Yup", "if he keeps this up..."

"Who'd ya think's gonna reach the Super Bowl?", "We..ell, Ah reckon"

Etc.

This can go on for hours, with all parties involved, quite happy/ unconcerned that the exact subject and statements were ran out last Saturday, and will be run through again next Saturday!

Sometimes we Past-time with a specific person, sometimes we prefer Past-timing in groups.

Sometimes we Past-time about as specific issue; sometimes we prefer a range of topics/ subjects.

Past-timing with hobbies or interests is usually harmless but can lead to misunderstandings.

Bitching can relieve pent-up emotions such as anger. Life is neither fair or unfair; but it can certainly *feel* unfair, as such bitching is a healthy way to feel better.

Past-timing can be cruel and devastating in the "gossip" mode.

In fact in Gossip mode people will quite happily repeat half-truths and slander someone else without ever checking their facts. Unfortunately new *gossips* will take such slander as the "gospel truth", perhaps even adding their own juicy little twist, when gossiping with others.
The more "near the knuckle" or OTT the gossip is, the higher the Stroke generation. Each gasp of disbelief from their audience adding at least twice the number of generated Strokes.
An innocent victim of gossiping could be ignored, vilified, dropped from the social scene, even "ran out of town". If they run a business they could be forced out of business just by rumours they may never be aware of.

Whilst every gossip believes implicitly in what they are saying and that they have the right to say such things. Although they could be sued for slander most gossips are sly creatures that ensure their particular clique of gossips are well under their control. I.e. they would not betray their source since their source of gossip is also their source of Strokes. "So what! If their life is destroyed; surely they must have deserved it?", "After all if they hadn't…… then we wouldn't have….", "We gossips couldn't all be wrong could we? Tee hee!", "Somebody has to watch out for these things!", etc.

Sick isn't it? Yet every gossip will quite happily run down *bitchers* and *hobbyists* without the slightest idea that bitching and past-timing about hobbies/ interests is relatively harmless. Whilst their gossiping can tear apart marriages, families, communities, etc.

P.P. P.'s

- Strokes are the unconscious mind's measurement of both our existence and survival.

- Strokes affect **every** part of Transactional Analysis.

- Strokes begin as physical touches/ feelings and as we develop they can also be words, gestures, etc.

- A shortage of Strokes creates the unconscious belief that we are dying. The Adult switches off, as the Child and/ or Parent becomes reactive.

- Excess Strokes create euphoria, even "spiritual" experiences.

- Disassociation [i.e. Sleep, day dreaming, reading, etc.] *feels* safe to the unconscious mind, but give the lowest performance in Stroke generation.

- Intimacy [i.e. genuine shared feelings and thoughts.] "Feels" unsafe to the unconscious mind, yet gives the highest performance in Stroke generation.

- In infants insufficient Strokes leads to a condition known as *Marasmus*, where the body either "wastes away" or fails to develop.

- Insufficient Strokes in early childhood also affects emotional and psychological development.

- There are three types of Stroke: Positive, Negative and Plastic; also known as warm fuzzy's, cold prickly's and plastic.

- There are three degrees of Stroke generation/ loss.

- Physical contact such as a massage or aromatherapy, is a good source of Strokes.

LIFE POSITIONS

Each of us adopts a "life position" in our early childhood. These are also referred to as the "OK positions".

Internally we measure our *value* as human beings, both within ourselves and through the reactions/ behaviour/ attitude of the people around us; when we are very young children.

If that value is high then we adopt an OK position, perceiving that we have value to both ourselves and to others. Thought processes/ decisions/ attitudes all reflect this internal value.

However if that value is low then we adopt a not OK position, perceiving that we have little or no value to both ourselves and to others. Again thought processes/ decisions/ attitudes all reflect this internal value. To be not OK is devastating, our entire lives can be spent believing that everyone is better [in some way] than we are. That others are more *valuable* therefore their needs come first. We can be prone to anxiety/ depression/ addictive behaviour/ obsessive behaviour/ psychosomatic disorders/ etc.

We need to be loved [*valued*] yet often **reject** compliments/ value statements/ love/ etc. through a not OK belief, that we are intrinsically unworthy. Mistakenly believing that if others could see us through our eyes they would realise how hopeless we truly are. Mistakenly believing that such compliments/ love/ etc. are either cruel jokes to wind us up; or that the people giving such compliments are very kind/ generous perhaps even pitying us.
Support/ care given to us in good faith is rejected because every part of our being **knows** that there has been some mistake and that they [the carer] doesn't really know **us**.

Our lives are filled with lack of confidence, low self-esteem, low self worth, fear and anxiety. Tasks/ adventures others accept so easily appear insurmountable to ourselves. In deeper degrees of not OK-ness even every day tasks can seem impossible or fraught with danger.

As we cannot believe that we worth anything, we can rarely identify a partner that will truly care for and support us.

Without choice, without hope we exist from day to day, perhaps going from one religion to another, one self-help book to another, one partner to another; never quite believing, never understanding.

If **you** recognise *yourself* in this book, **don't** buy another until you have read and applied everything you can get from this book. This time **get it right**! To put it crudely/ bluntly just because your unconscious mind felt you were the lowest creature/ vermin/ scum on earth, when you were a child; does not mean that you need to be that now!

Take the "please wipe your feet/ kick me/ etc." sign off your back!

Take back your birth right; **you were born OK** [even if there is a physical disability, or extreme poverty, or you were left as an orphan, or whatever].

It is up to **you** to reclaim your birthright!

Another book, a new religion, a new partner, another qualification, or whatever *you* are chasing will not reclaim this for you. Only you can give you, your OK-ness back.

[Although this is a "what is it?" book, rather than a "how to" book; there is enough information and direction in this book for you to begin to change! Don't wait to be rescued! Don't let yourself down! This time you can get it right! Go for it; make yourself a contract that from today no matter what program you received in your childhood, you will change/ move forward. Take yourself from where you are now and move forward, until every part of your being becomes OK. Then; if you still want to look for your new partner, religion, self help book/ guru, etc. you can.
*However, the chances are you'll be too busy **enjoying** your life to go back to chasing rescuers and dreams!*]

Not OK-ness is a never-ending cycle of missed: opportunities, chances, hopes and dreams. Fed by anxiety, fear, low self-esteem, low self worth and bouts of melancholy; until we die unfulfilled with one last "if only" on our lips.

The OK position gives us life.

In OK-ness lie hopes, dreams, self worth; achievements abound and life becomes easy. OK-ness is to living, as not OK-ness is to existing.
The original Life position is chosen through the unconscious Child based on how we *feel*. Ultimately we can choose the final Life position through rational thought in the Adult.

Whilst it is possible to find the final position naturally, it is generally accepted that a period of therapy/ trauma/ understanding/ or introspection is required to review the Life positions.

There are four Life positions these being :-

1. I'm not OK – You're OK

2. I'm not OK – You're not OK

3. I'm OK – You're not OK

4. **I'm OK – You're OK**

Position 1. I'm not OK – You're OK, is created within the **Child** where an unconscious decision is made that the internal Child is not OK but that the adults around that child are.

Basically the internal Child *feels* bad or awful; but accepts Strokes and other incoming data from the adults around it.

Although unconscious this *is* a decision. A decision based on feeling without recognisable rational thought. Whilst the decision can be altered obviously the *original* events and *original* feelings connected to those events cannot. Traditionally this position lends itself to neurosis/ anxiety and certain types of addictive behaviour and/ or depression

Feelings connected to the "Not OK" position are present time, negative, and unless consciously aware, fixed. However, these feelings can be altered either through conscious choice [using knowledge and being consistent!], understanding [and acceptance], or through a counselling/ hypnotherapeutic process.

Any of these can automatically "upgrade" the position, to an OK position.

You did read correctly: - "the *original* events and *original* feelings..." hinting that whilst the original events and feelings cannot be altered, that your perception of the events and feelings connected to the Not OK decision can be changed.

We do this naturally [but rarely] as we look back to the past and *remember* things slightly differently from our shared participants. Our parents [if they remember our significant events at all?] have a different perception of what occurred to our perception. Older/ younger siblings also *remember* such occasions quite differently to our own perceptions.

Unless addressed these Life Positions (LP) affect us for the rest of our lives. The LP dictates our susceptibility to symptoms, emotions, choices, etc. Obviously a positive internal LP affects us positively, whilst a negative internal LP affects us negatively. Position 1. Is a negative internal LP (although also being a positive External LP.).

Symptoms of position 1 are a need for approval/ recognition/ acceptance from others, internal anxiety type dialogues ["what ifs?, why me's?, etc.], psychosomatic conditions and even depression in severe cases.

People in position 1 will usually adopt the "Flight" mode in stress if possible [using the "Fight" response as a last resort]; presenting/ clinical symptoms include general anxiety, lack of confidence, low self esteem, phobia's, obsessive behaviour, psychosomatic illnesses, IBS, ME, displacement activity, repeated Scripts, etc.

Position 2. I'm OK – You're not OK, is created within the **Parent** where an unconscious decision is made that the internal Parent is OK but that adults around the child are not. *[Remember lower case initial = actual child, or their parents, or the adults around them. Upper case initial = Parent, Adult and Child minds.]*

Basically the internal Parent *knows* it is right, whilst refusing to accept some Strokes and other incoming data from the adults around it.

The same rules apply in that this is a decision and can be altered; however it can be considerably more difficult [but not impossible] to assist someone in this position to move forward. Traditionally this position lends itself to "psychosis" [especially where developing Frames of Reference are affected] and certain types of criminal behaviour.

Symptoms of position 2 may include a **total** belief of self-righteousness, disregard for social authority [i.e. Police, judges, etc.], usually driven to go "their own way", often disregard others safety or needs, etc.

Position 3. I'm not OK – You're not OK, is created within the Child **and** Parent, where an unconscious decision is made where neither the internal Child or the incoming data from adults around the developing infant is acceptable. Occasionally this position is adopted from birth! Traditionally this position may lend itself to certain types of autism and epilepsy [idiopathic, particularly versions of petit mal, where loss of concentration, awareness, or consciousness are linked].

Symptoms of position 3 usually include periods of disassociation. These can be psychological [excessive day dreaming, inability to focus on external stimuli such as lessons at school, switching off, and in more intense cases autism or idiopathic epilepsy.], and/ or physical [inability to socialise, withdrawing from contact with others, hiding in personal refuges such as a tree house or under the stairs, etc.]. NB Whilst the original position is technically an unconscious decision, the symptoms are an automatic consequence of that decision. I.e. once the position is adopted the individual has little or no choice over the symptoms. This is common for all of the Life Positions.

Position 4. I'm OK – You're OK, is rare in western society as a natural or childhood response. This position is usually worked at consciously through the Adult and within reason requires regular updating. Any of the previous positions can be worked at until position 4 is achieved. This position is the optimum for good mental health and stability. In fact many additional factors [Scripts, Stamp Collecting, etc.] have considerably less effect on the individual, once I'm OK – You're OK is achieved.
Life Trauma's, stress, social changes, etc. can return the individual back to their original position. However a modest amount of effort will retrieve the situation bringing an I'm OK – You're OK position once again.

Symptoms of position 4 are feeling comfortable within our self. Life is seen in it's true perspective and an ability to enjoy life is prevalent. Basically we begin to live rather than exist!

The Adult mind is easier to access, whilst Child and Parent drives are reasonable.

The Life Positions are created throughout our early childhood. The creation and perceptions of our Child and Parent minds usually dictate the Life Position we adopt.

If we *feel* loved and cared for in our Child minds then an internal OK position is likely.

If we *feel* rejected, unloved, etc. then an internal Not OK position is adopted.

These positions have little to do with our parents intent since they could beat us constantly, tease us constantly, etc. and provided we *feel* loved and cared for we will adopt the I'm OK position. However our parents could attempt to meet our every whim, being constantly vigilant and loving; if we *feel* unloved we will still adopt the I'm Not OK position.

During our early development we are purely mammalian rather than human; but parents continue to treat their young children as miniature human beings. It is primarily this process that tends to cause the mis-perception that we are unloved.

Choices are often offered to young children then ignored. The inability to recognise the passage of time in young infants is a source of humour for parents but not addressed! Promises are made but not kept. Etc.

Of course we parents have the excuse that our parents did this to us. "My parents beat me if I was bad, it never did me any harm!"; therefore suggesting that corporal punishment is correct in all cases.

Yes our parents inadvertently programmed us with our own Life Positions, as did their parents programme them. But that doesn't make it right. These are excuses, enabling us to do nothing, to avoid change.

[As you learn more of yourself through this book, you can take responsibility for your own happiness and mental stability. Then you can offer this to your own children; lead by example. If you are genuinely happy and carefree, then the people around you can become happier and more carefree.]

However if you nag constantly, shout at your children, lose your temper, ignore your children, change the rules to suit yourself, put yourself first, etc. then your children may adopt the external You're Not OK position.

You are risking their mental, physical, social, future; purely because you can't be bothered to fix yourself! Yes life can be hard, yes situations change, perhaps you really didn't get the chances you deserved in life; but don't use these excuses to mess up your children's lives!

At least have the guts to own up and admit that **you** aren't/ didn't care properly for your children. Perhaps it was out of spite because you felt your parents didn't care for you! Perhaps you really didn't know, and the lack of care and support for your children was unconscious. Perhaps you are a PC'er! Surely true Political Correctness should mean that **both** parents find the best nurturing environment for their children; whereas today it appears to mean: stuff the kids we're both entitled to have careers, be fulfilled, be selfish, etc. a stranger can look after the children, if we have any?

Practitioner Warning

Whilst the intent of TA is to allow self-responsibility and an opportunity for improvement; some therapists/ counsellors/ psychologists/ psychiatrists actually push people deeper or back into an unsuitable Life Position. Going back over past issues **regardless** of whether this is done consciously or through an altered state of consciousness [hypnosis, psychotropic drugs such as barbiturates/ hypnotics, certain types of religious ceremony, etc.] **will** affect the Life Position. Where positive feelings are accessed or negative feelings are over written with positive feelings then the patient will gravitate toward an OK position. However where negative feelings are constantly explored, or worse still positive feelings are inadvertently re-written as negative feelings, then the patient will gravitate toward a Not OK position.

This is true for **internalised** OK positions. Usually it is true of **externalised** OK positions, however some aspects of externalised OK positions are **learned** rather than **experienced**, as such therapists/ psychiatrists should be particularly cautious when assisting in altering an **external** OK position.

Although the Frames of Reference section is merely a taster for the general public, any practitioner dealing with issues of emotional/ mental health should have a thorough understanding of that particular section. Accepting that a facial expression, gesture, throw away comment, etc. can have a devastating and even permanent effect on their patient! Since an apparent dismissal of a Frame of Reference **or** the acceptance of an inappropriate Frame of Reference by an authority figure is adopted instantly and **unconsciously** by the patient, this can make or break the chosen Life Position.

P.P.P.'s

- There are four life positions:-

1. I'm not OK – You're OK

2. I'm OK – You're not OK

3. I'm not OK – You're not OK

4. **I'm OK – You're OK**

- Positions 1 to 3 are **unconscious** choices, requiring no further effort to implement.

- Positions 1 to 3 are often adopted in early childhood.

- Position 4 is usually a **conscious** choice, requiring understanding and effort to implement and maintain.

- Position 4 is often addressed in adulthood.

- The positions are normally adopted through a series of *feelings* connected to childhood events.

- The *original* events and feelings cannot be altered.

- Both the memories of the events and the feelings connected [in present time] to those events can be altered.

- Obviously where memories/ feelings are altered; if negative then we gravitate towards a Not OK position, if positive then we gravitate towards an OK position.

- People are **born OK**; but through the process of childhood often adopt a not OK position.

- OK is far more intense than just being all right or fine. It is the unconscious minds' interpretation of our total self worth [our *value* as a human being]. OK is our belief that we are valued by others, as well as being worthwhile in ourselves.

- Life Positions are founded on many events in our lives, as such modifying one memory/ feeling may have little and/ or short-term effects.

- *Understanding,* that events and perception of those events in early childhood are usually common throughout each culture/ society, and often represent a misperception of childhood can affect many memories/ feelings and may have considerable and/ or long-term effects. [i.e. Just reading and understanding this book can begin to create positive changes to *your* life positions.]

- The Life Positions adopted dictate the general behaviour patterns in life.

[Whilst it is possible to carry out criminal behaviour in any of the life positions, criminal behaviour is more common in the I'm OK, You're not OK position. Anxiety and depression are more common in the You're OK, I'm not OK position, etc.]

- Each Life Position has it's own preferences for different types of Scripts, Game Playing, Stamp collecting, etc.

- Due to lack of research it is not known whether the I'm OK, You're OK position can be adopted permanently [i.e. without further/ continued work] or whether it is something that once having attained it, it must be regularly monitored/ topped up.

GAME PLAYING

Game Playing is a strange term since it implies that some form of fun, recreation or other pleasurable past time is involved.

Game Playing is a nickname in Transactional Analysis for a process [usually unconscious] of stealing/ mugging/ taking Strokes from someone else.

For academic purposes "Game Playing" is a useful term, you can analyse the opening move, note the development of play and identify the concluding action. All of which gives a fairly benign impression of Game Playing.

In real life [i.e. *Your* life!] Game Playing is an insidious cancer that will eat away at you, your relationships, your friends, your work, etc.

*Game Playing is **not** a game! Game Playing is **not** a game!! Game Playing is **not** a game!!!*

You are playing games when you Game Play, but it is not a game.

In a true game a person or a team usually win or draw, whilst the other person or team loses or draws. It is expected that each participant has *chosen* to play. In some cases players are paid $/ £1,000,000's per season for professional sports. Other than by accident no one is expected to die. None of the players would normally lose their family, partner, etc. if they lost the game/ match. But above, all the actual game itself is expected to be **fair**. That each team should have an equal chance of winning. If it didn't then we often root for the "under-dogs" since it is understood that they are playing a team in a "different league".

At no point in modern sports would we accept or enjoy a mis-match or unfairness within the rules. Imagine if the next time your favourite team play they had to wear 20lb weights around each ankle, whilst the opposing team didn't! Or you favourite tennis player had to wear 20lb weights on their wrists and ankles, whilst the other player didn't! Or in the next Olympic Games the U.S.A. and Great Britain had a 20% penalty on times, weights, distances, etc. that no other team had to put up with!

Would that be fair? Would you consider it a game any more?

Yet this is exactly how Game Playing progresses: -

1. The opposing *player* may not choose to play, but they will be made to play anyway.

2. The first player decides the type of game.

3. The first player decides the rules of play.

4. The first player sets suitable handicaps on the opposing player to ensure that the first player wins every time.

5. Every time you lose you **die** a bit. If you lose big time you die a lot.

6. Third degree Game Playing can involve court proceedings, divorce, prison, serious harm and death.

7. The first player may be so far beyond your league, that you wouldn't stand a chance, yet they will still "sucker" you into a game if they feel like it!

8. Professional Game Players will quite happily "sucker" the dying into a game that only the professional game player will ever win.

9. Of course some of the best [Professional game players], are those that *appear* to be disadvantaged or dying.

10. No one is exempt!

I would prefer to think of Game Playing as compulsory mugging. In fact the title might have been better served as Mugging.

[Mugging: - To rob/ steal with violence often in a public place]

The person initiating the mugging almost always takes the Stroke/ s. They use every tactic available and **take** the Stroke/ s. There is no mercy, clemency, appeal, fair play, etc. When the mugging is initiated theft of the Stroke/ s is usually swift and merciless.

Professional muggers/ game players are sometimes **so** swift that it is not until they have left, that you may realise you were mugged!

*In Game Playing there are only the **mugger/s** and the **victim/s**.*

*There is no honour in taking part, no heroic struggle, just the winner [mugger] and a loser [victim]. Cruel, usually swift, occasionally violent [psychologically], barbaric. A game? Perhaps in its broadest sense, but never, never assume that it's **just** a game. This is a crocodile dragging down and tearing apart a day old baby zebra; no remorse, no regret, no mercy, this is survival of the fittest at its worst!*

Most people are unaware that they play games, or that someone else is playing games with them.

In the game you are drawn in by a statement, gesture or action. [Referred to in TA as the "con".]

The first player Says loudly "oh no!". [The con]

You reveal your "Gimmick", this is usually a driver in a Script* A rule or phrase usually Parental, or a feeling/ emotional driver in the Child. I.e. I **must** help you because I'm your wife/ husband/ mother/ father/ daughter/ etc.

You respond "what's wrong?", but mentally you think how can I help? [Referred to as the response]

At this stage the "what's wrong" [*how can I help?*] responses can run for seconds, minutes, hours, days, weeks, months or even years. Until you are unable to assist or advise the initial player any further. Usually the con/ gimmick routine repeats itself until the second player "fails".

Then a "switch" is pulled. The first player makes a statement at which point the both players feel confused/ surprised [this is referred to as the crossup]. Almost immediately both players feel another emotional charge. The first player usually feels a Parental self-righteousness type of feeling, perhaps thinking "see I knew you couldn't help me!"; whilst the second player usually feels a Child "down/ not OK" type feeling, perhaps even depressed. [This is referred to as the "Payoff".]
*See Glossary and the chapter entitled Scripts.

This creates a game formula#: -

Con + Gimmick = Response -> Switch -> Crossup -> Payoff

As I mentioned earlier this is great fun for practitioners who can analyse the Game formula to their hearts content. Which of course leads to another practitioner habit: Past-timing [hopefully in the shared interest mode rather than the gossip mode.] about clients and TA. What is particularly attractive to some practitioners is that TA at this level has it's own language, so only the "experts" know what you are talking about! Thereby keeping this particular form of Past-timing very select.

So why have I placed all of this complicated formula business in a "common sense" book? You may ask?

You didn't ask? Sorry I'm going to tell you anyway!

The Gimmick usually borders on the unconscious or is so habitual that we very rarely recognise it. Since this book is supposed to help you to help yourself; I can hardly suggest that you find a specialist to help you to identify **your** particular Games and Gimmicks?

However, the **Payoff** feelings are usually noticeable and since Games are usually repetitive, all you need to do is look for a regular situation where you feel negative/ down/ angry/ hurt/ etc. immediately after or while you are with someone else!

When you recognise this you can either work your way back through the formula until you can change something [i.e. the response or your gimmick] or you can disassociate/ keep away/ disconnect from that person.

It can be this simple! We all know someone that no matter how hard we try with them; not only do things not change but some how: - we *feel* that it's our fault, or we *feel* as if we have let them down, or we *feel* put upon, or we *feel* hurt, or whatever?
If this is happening then you are involved in Game playing. Go back three paragraphs!
#Initial concepts of TA including Game Playing and the Game Formula were developed by Dr. Eric Berne (1910 – 1970)

If the *feelings* on the previous page seem familiar, you must **change** your activity/ response/ contact, if you want things to improve.

A familiar theme in therapy: if you try harder at what you are doing you get more of what you have got! Simple as that! Change or accept, it's your choice?

If you are on the victim end of Game Playing, the harder you try the more painful it will get. The Game will deteriorate into Second then Third Degree, you **will** get hurt, then seriously hurt. The person playing Games with you [whether it is your mother/ father, brother/ sister, manager/ subordinate, husband/ wife, etc.] doesn't give a damn for you at that moment; **no matter what they say**. In fact it is usually **what** they are saying that is dragging you into the Game!

If you **truly** want to avoid the *feelings*/ Game; <u>you</u> **must** change something that you are doing, until the Game collapses and stops.

Identify the *feelings*/ Payoff, and then go back through the formula until you find a part of it you can change. Then change it. [Of course if you are dealing with a Professional, you will quite rapidly find yourself back in the same situation. So persevere. Go back through the formula again, and again, and again, until the Game collapses. Even seasoned Professionals will give up if the Game constantly fails to reach its climax.

Remember the crocodile, it cannot eat the baby zebra if it [the zebra] goes to a different watering hole. The crocodile will choose a different prey.

Remember the crocodile, regardless of how close or important the Game player is to you, **they are the crocodile, <u>you</u>** are the baby zebra - dead meat - easy prey - history.

I cannot emphasise this enough, since most people refuse to believe it!

If **your** mother is a third degree Professional Game Player, she will play the Game to **your death**. The Game is played not **to the death** [in some honourable Gladiatorial style] but to **your** death.

If your son is a third degree Professional Game Player, he will play the Game to **your death**. Blood is not *thicker than water*, to the crocodile blood *tastes better than water*, family is fair game to the Professional.

There are no exceptions.

P.P.P.'S

- Game playing is not [in any civilised understanding] a game.

- Game Playing steals Strokes.

- If you are drawn into a Game you **will** lose.

- Game Playing would be easier to recognise if it was thought of as Mugging.

- The Mugger has no thought or concern for the victim.

- Game Playing is the Law of the Jungle, reflect for a moment on " *a crocodile dragging down and tearing apart a day old baby zebra; no remorse, no regret, no mercy, this is survival of the fittest at its worst!* ".

- Professional Game players often spend their entire lives mugging people, even complete strangers! But prefer people they know.

- A Professional can be so skilful that you may not realise you've been mugged until after they have gone.

- Most people play Games, where they are first degree there is rarely any harm, where they are second degree they cause considerable distress to others, and where third degree is involved they are played "for keeps". [Victims of third degree Game Playing end up in psychiatric care/ divorce/ court/ prison/ commit suicide/ etc. Remember there is no mercy, the first Player will push the Game to its final and horrifying climax **regardless** of whether **you** wanted to play in the first place!]

- Professional Game Players will usually deny any involvement/ interest/ etc. in Game Playing. Often claiming a pseudo-legitimate excuse as to why they must "get divorced"/ "take them to court"/ etc. If the victim commits suicide the Professional Player will have lots of pseudo-legitimate excuses that distance them from the victims actions "s/he always was highly strung"/ "I always said s/he would do something like this one day"/ "oh! Isn't it terrible, I wonder what could have caused him/ her to do such a thing?"/ "I was always there for her/ him, why didn't they come to me?"/ etc.

- If you truly want to avoid the *feelings*/ Game, **you** must change something that you are doing. Don't wait for the other person to change, that is part of the Game!

- The solution is to Cause the Game to collapse and stop.

- Find the *feelings*, then go back through the Formula, until you identify something **you** can change, then change it.

- **Remember** the crocodile cannot eat the baby zebra if it isn't there; your emergency solution is to cut off contact with the Game player. **Remember you** are the baby zebra - dead meat - easy prey - "dead man walking" - history.

- Professional Players often prefer the blood of relatives/ lovers/ partners to that of work colleagues or strangers.

- There are a handful of positive Games; if you must Game Play use those. But remember a Professional Player can turn a positive Game into a negative Game in seconds. **You** won't realise until it's too late, so be careful.

- There are no exceptions.

You may have noticed that Game Playing was relatively short. It also appeared full of doom and destruction. The names, types and details of the Games are missing.

There are several reasons for this:-

- Most of W3M™ has been drawn from short tutorial sessions I given my clients over the past twelve years [over 12,000 hours of 1-2-1].
- During this period where possible I've given a light/ easy introduction into that particular part of TA that would help their situation/ condition then recommended a suitable book.
- Where said book was comprehensive, easy to read, meets their needs and was easily available; I recommended it.

Unfortunately many of these books are now out of print, or so dated as to be practically useless. Where these books are out of date I would have explored that particular aspect of TA in more depth.
One book I still recommend is:-

Games People Play
By
Eric Berne, M.D.

ISBN 0-14-002768-8

Here you will find Life Games, Marital Games, Party Games, Sexual Games, Underworld Games, Consulting Room Games, Good Games, etc.

Finally I don't normally teach Game Playing in the type of clinic work I accept, as such I could not have done justice to the subject.

If I attempted to cover Game Playing in any detail, I would need fifty more pages, also there is little new insight I could have offered, sorry ☹. What I chose to do instead was emphasise the severity and ruthlessness of negative Game Playing. [This is a new insight, drawn directly from clinical practise!] After all, one of the reasons W3M™ **is unique** is that many of the chapters of TA have been given completely **new** insights and interpretations.

If you would like to know more about Game Playing, please read Eric Berne's book.

PLEASURE

We are clearly not designed to be in our Adult mind constantly nor are we designed to constantly have thoughts running through our consciousness. Most forms of stress, anxiety and depression involve excessive and/or irrational conscious thought. We all require on a daily basis "time out" in such a way that our mind and body can repair and replenish itself. Where we are suffering from stress, anxiety or depression, this interferes with our normal sleep processes. At these times this "time out" becomes essential. For the purpose of this book, the nature of this time out is referred to as "Free pleasure". This phrase is used to identify the difference between "Free pleasure" and "Adapted pleasure".

Free Pleasure

Free pleasure is any form of pleasure where the recognition of or feelings of pleasure are received in the "here and now". Free pleasure is a natural condition/ state located or felt in the Child mind.

There are two distinctly different forms of Free pleasure these being "active and passive".

In "active" Free pleasure the feelings of pleasure are gained through activity where the person involved may become completely absorbed by that activity. This could be drawing, painting, playing a musical instrument or any absorbing process [usually creative but not always].
Where pleasure is created through being totally immersed/ absorbed in the activity; as opposed to Adapted Pleasure where pleasure is gained from the end result.

In "passive" Free pleasure, the feelings of pleasure are gained through inactivity where the person involved is completely absorbed in "chilling out" or "switching off". This could be sunbathing, daydreaming, meditation or hypnosis where there is no particular end product or active process that is required.

Basically, all one is required to do is switch off. This allows the body and mind to adopt the optimum position for self-repair. This period is essential for both physical and mental health and is required on a **daily** basis.

Free pleasure is the true/ honest feeling that allows the Child mind to assess the *value* in feeling terms of that activity/ inactivity, **whilst** experiencing that activity/ inactivity. I.e. You are sun bathing, whilst you are sun bathing you feel good. Your Child has assessed the value of sun bathing at that particular time on that particular day.

During periods of Free pleasure the repair/ healing/ immune systems of the body and the digestive processes, work far more effectively.

Adapted Pleasure

Adapted pleasure is located primarily within the Parent mind but awareness is shared with the Child.

Although a natural reaction in the Stress response located through the "Flight or Fight" reaction, this is learned/ trained/ harnessed until feelings of relief become feelings of pleasure, thus perverting the normal condition.

Adapted pleasure is any form of pleasure where the recognition of, or feelings of pleasure are gained through competitiveness (facing death and surviving), taking risks or productiveness. As a general rule, most people in Western Society tend to use Adapted Pleasure rather than Free Pleasure.

During the Adapted Pleasure process, feelings are displaced [anger, anxiety, frustration, etc. are the usual choices, assuming that all receipt of feeling has not been closed down, which is a common alternative], until the end of the activity.

Adapted Pleasure is a perversion, often becoming the source of many perversions whether sexual or otherwise in adult life. The use of such an emotive term [perversion] is justified in the sheer hell the average person goes through because of Adapted Pleasure. Since the level of anxiety/ pain involved in achieving pleasure is usually equal to or greater than the actual amount of pleasure received. Unfortunately the more the individual experiences stroke loss, anxiety and pain from this process, the harder they will try to gain pleasure from the Adapted Pleasure route, constantly leading to ever greater distress.

At the time of writing this, it is primarily the educational system in both the UK and the USA that encourages the replacement of healthy Free Pleasure with the perverted Adapted pleasure. This is via a hidden agenda of target-orientated assessment and production values.

[People trained to gain all their pleasure through Adapted rather than Free generally make good workers, but are much more likely to be affected by stress. Where people are allowed to retain Free pleasure they are less likely to adopt the "Protestant work ethic". However, they are much more likely to be stress proof and generally happier with life.]

Although there are several different types of Adapted Pleasure, some of these being risk taking, competitiveness and productiveness, they are often combined. But to the unconscious mind there are different types of chemical releases connected to each.

In risk taking/ competitiveness, as perceived through the unconscious mind, we have in some way [no matter how small] faced death and survived. This is regardless of whether we are actively racing a motor-cycle or playing a game of squash.

The greater the risk/ competitiveness the more intense the feeling of pleasure on surviving/ winning.

In a true life-threatening situation, perhaps being caught at the front of an avalanche while skiing; we may not be the first person to reach safety, but we will still share in and enjoy the powerful feelings of pleasure of knowing that we made it.

Whereas in a game such as squash where perhaps the only true likelihood of death is a stroke or heart attack and this is relatively slim (in comparison to the avalanche), it is in the winning that the greater sensation of pleasure is received. Even this can be reduced if we perceive that our competitor has relatively poor skills at which point we begin to compete against ourselves. The sheer physical effort and the anxiety involved if we lose and/ or are losing usually outweigh the short period of pleasure we gain from the activity. Also where there is a true threat to our survival then it is often only a matter of time before physical injury or even death occurs, since the unconscious mind encourages greater and greater risk to gain the original intensity of pleasure.

Although it is difficult to see how much pleasure we could gain and enjoy from an act of stupidity once we are dead; we still seem to throw ourselves headlong into dangerous situations once we have developed this particular type of risk orientated Adapted Pleasure.

Adapted Pleasure through productiveness usually involves structuring our activities and time in an effort to produce something. Whilst this is normally something tangible such as a physical object, occasionally it could be as ethereal as a suntan [obviously in this case sun bathing would not be a Free Pleasure activity].

Whilst this process often begins prior to school, it appears to be the direction and intent of the educational process to establish Adapted Pleasure [in particular through productiveness] as a replacement for Free Pleasure.

*After all, we can hardly have people actually **enjoying happiness**, when we could have them "doing something" instead.*

The process begins with a task to be completed during a lesson. As we master this, we are given a task to be completed during the day. This gradually changes to a task to be completed during the week/ term/ year and even over two years. Grades have to be achieved, exams have to be passed, homework and projects have to be completed. In the UK system where GCSEs are the culmination of two years work, it is obvious that there is two years worth of homework, lessons, tests, projects, mock exams and finally the actual exams themselves. This actually involves two years worth of worry and anxiety becoming more acute as the examination date arrives. So much so, that many children become ill or commit suicide, because of the build up and intensity of anxiety. Even after the exam there is still a high level of anxiety as the results are awaited.

Sadly as if there were not enough casualties from this process, the whole thing is repeated over the following two years with GCSE A'levels.

Finally, University arrives and we get the opportunity to repeat the whole process over another three years with yet more nervous breakdowns, addictive behaviour, dropouts and suicides.

The pleasure we gain from passing these exams is usually short lived.

81

Perhaps, although unintentionally, this can be the result of parental interference. I.e. you pass nine out of ten GCSEs with a reasonable grade failing Maths, English, Chemistry, or whatever. Your parents may say something along the lines of "What happened to Maths?" This can leave you with the feeling that you have somehow failed. You may ignore the fact that you have achieved 90% of the target you set out for. Quite often we [as are our parents] are perfectly happy with 90% grades yet for some odd reason will fail to recognise that this is the true result of the above example.

Perhaps if we applied for a job our prospective employer may look at our exam results and with much huffing and puffing, explain how they were hoping to have someone with A'level passes rather than just basic GCSEs. End of interview. All feelings of pleasure that we may have gained from a nine out of ten pass rate have vanished into thin air since ultimately we haven't made the grade.

What we are often unaware of is our friends, who may have continued with their education and gained their A'levels, may have gone through a similar interview where they are now told that their prospective employer was hoping for someone with a Degree rather than just A'levels.

Even if we go through the University process not just achieving a degree but perhaps a Masters or Ph.D. we may now be informed that we are over-qualified during our job interviews. What we are unaware of is that these are **pseudo-legitimate excuses** used by interviewers to try and let the candidate down lightly.

There is no reason to assume that because someone left school after their GCSEs, they are not capable of learning and carrying out a job that might be presumed suitable for someone with A'levels. The guidelines laid down for interview processes for employers are usually subjective anyway. As it not usually the **knowledge** that will be required by the Company for someone that had achieved A'level standard, but the evidence that the person was prepared to put the two years worth of work into taking and passing the A'levels in the first place.

Yet this is exactly what a person would have done in taking the ordinary GCSEs.

Because so many of the influential years of our lives are taken up in learning Adapted Pleasure, we often forget how to have or enjoy Free Pleasure. This tends to mean that we choose hobbies, activities and interests that use Adapted rather than Free Pleasure.

Ultimately, this means we use exactly the same mechanism to unwind and relax as we use at work that caused the need for us to unwind and relax in the first place.

Eventually this will fail and we will either anxiete, compensate or die.

Many people begin to worry habitually and excessively through this process, those of us who don't have usually compensated in some way.

Perhaps we smoke or use alcohol or street drugs or even eat to excess. We may even just sit for hours in front of the television in a vain attempt to compensate. Those people who don't anxiete or compensate in a meaningful way will eventually have a stroke or heart attack or may even develop a chronic condition purely from Adapted Pleasure.

Yet these same people are often quite judgmental when they look at other cultures and/or people that enjoy Free Pleasure [feeling perhaps that it is wrong to just enjoy life]. Possibly thinking or even saying: - "They can't do that forever", "If they wanted to work they would find work", "It's all right for them! They don't have a mortgage/ children/ *whatever* to support.", "You can't spend your entire life enjoying life!", etc. [*Why not?* Ed.]

Remember it is the intent of the education system to replace Free Pleasure with Adapted since our education system is primarily designed to produce good workers rather than educate us.

After all, if the system were designed to educate us, then we would be taught the things that we need to know.

It is part of human life that we expect to survive our parents and grandparents, as such we need to know how to cope with bereavement and grieve adequately.

We would normally expect to share our lives with a partner perhaps eventually having children, therefore we need to know how to choose a good partner and how to bring up our children.

We are affected emotionally and psychologically through the process of childhood. Therefore we need to learn how to grow beyond that so that we may reach our true potential.

We normally expect to work for a living and therefore need to know how to get the job we want and how to continue enjoying that job for almost 50 years.

We need to know how to get on with the people around us and to avoid arguments and disharmony with our partners.

__All__ of these issues are essential for happiness, good mental health, and well being. They are also important for the health of the Nation/ Society.

Yet few if any of these things are taught __adequately__ through our present educational system.

Adapted pleasure is best suited to "Capitalistic/ materialistic" types of society. Allowing society and the wealthy to benefit the most while suffering the least, whereas the individual and the poor/ dispossessed benefit least, whilst suffering the most.

Since many "street" drugs mimic the Adapted Pleasure process it is hardly surprising that the most dissatisfied/ disadvantaged tend to use the more addictive drugs.

Generally Adapted Pleasure in small amounts is relatively harmless, but if used as the main source of pleasure can lead to stress/ anxiety/ depression/ addictive behaviour/ even death. Again this is remarkably similar to the use of many types of "street" drugs.

Finally Adapted Pleasure is supported by the misperception that one or both of your parents didn't love you, or that you are intrinsically bad, or [if this is different from the first two issues] you have adopted the Not OK position. Yet just accepting that these are misperceptions can often break the Adapted Pleasure cycle.

"Free pleasure is a natural condition/ state located or felt in the Child mind... You are sun bathing, whilst you arc sun bathing you feel good..." [Note the Shadow and the supporting "reality" is the Child; looking out from the darkness. Interesting perspective, Frank. Thank you. Ed.]

85

P.P.P.'s

- True pleasure (referred to as Free Pleasure) is located within the Child.

- Free Pleasure is the natural Condition/ State involving active and passive processes.

- In Free Pleasure the repair/ healing systems of the body, work more efficiently.

- Free Pleasure is an honest feeling for a real time activity.

- Day dreaming, meditation, hypnotic states, etc. create Free Pleasure.

- Adapted Pleasure is primarily located within the Parent, but awareness is usually in the Child.

- Adapted Pleasure is *learned* condition considered as a perversion.

- Productiveness, risk taking, competitive sports, pack behaviour (i.e. Supporters at a football match), etc. create Adapted Pleasure.

- Adapted Pleasure is a displaced feeling often felt towards the end or even after activity has taken place.

- As a general rule, Adapted Pleasure (mainly productiveness) creates as much if not more anxiety than pleasure, hence the term perversion.

- Adapted Pleasure is the hidden agenda in schools, colleges, universities, working environments, etc.

- As a general rule, Adapted Pleasure (Mainly competitiveness) becomes more intense the closer the **unconscious** mind perceived it faced death and survived.

- The part of the unconscious mind responsible for identifying Adapted Pleasure constant pushes the boundaries. Therefore the intensity of pleasure gained from a competitive sport is gradually reduced little or no pleasure is gained. To compensate the individual is required to constantly excel/ upgrade to gain the same feeling of pleasure.

- The previous point 'is also valid for productiveness where increasing workloads/ targets must be met to gain the original intensity of pleasure.

- Ditto risk taking regardless of whether it is financial, sexual, or directly life threatening, to gain the original intensity or pleasure the risk needs to be increased.

- Certain type of recreational/ illegal drugs use, mimics the Adapted Pleasure process.

- Adapted Pleasure in small amounts is completely harmless, but if used as the main source of pleasure can lead to stress/ anxiety/ depression/ death.

- Adapted Pleasure is best suited to "Capitalist/ materialistic" types of society, where society and the wealthy benefit most, whilst the individual and the poor/ dispossessed suffer most.

- Adapted Pleasure also relies on misperceiving that one or both of your parents didn't love you/ that some how you are intrinsically bad/ the Not OK position in the Child.

- In Adapted Pleasure the action/ "Fight" systems of the body work more efficiently.

SCRIPTS

What are scripts?

How do you recognise them?

How do they differ from game playing*

Specifically, where do they come from?

There are three classifications given to Scripts within TA: -

Winning, Banal, and Hamartic.

It may be easier to simply think of these as: -

Winning, Boring, and Losing.

From a very simple point of view: if you run *Winning Scripts* then those things that you desire most will regularly become part of your life. I.e. if you truly desire to be president of your own company, that is exactly where you will end up. However, if you truly wish to be a "beach bum" in Barbados, then that is where you will end up. *Both* of these examples are Winning Scripts in that the results meet the perceived desires.

People indulging in Winning Scripts are usually referred to as "Winners".

Banal/ *Boring Scripts* are both intermediary Scripts [allowing a change between Losing/ Winning] and a Script in their own right.

Boring Scripts are just that, few chances are taken, no one wants to "rock the boat". Daily activities become routine, from meals to interests.
Sadly even where a new hobby or interest is taken up this very rapidly becomes part of the routine. In fact the word *routine* is a very good way of describing a Boring Script, since there is a routine for everything and everything becomes its own routine.

When used positively Boring Scripts create a period of stability in life, where the foundations for new horizons can be laid.
* See Glossary

But where a Boring Script is adopted for life, we might as well be asleep or dead. It is in reference to this that people indulging in Boring Scripts are usually referred to as "Sleepers"# or in third degree as "Zombies".

Boring Scripts whilst being quite repetitive, do allow us to cope with life. We often move between scripts depending upon the level/ type of stress we are under and our Stroke* levels.

Boring Scripts are mostly chosen as an alternative to Winning or Losing Scripts.

It is rare for people to naturally jump from a Losing Script to a Winning Script. Normally some form of psychological growth/ awareness is required prior to such an enormous leap. Also a period of stability is often required before the drivers* used to support a Losing Script can be overcome.

All scripts are supported by drivers; remove the drivers, and the script collapses!

In case you missed that: -

All scripts are supported by drivers; remove the drivers, and the script collapses!

[Most of our psychological processes appear to be self-repairing; it should therefore be noted that until the *new* thought processes become habitual; the unconscious mind will attempt to replace the drivers. Also at any time in the future with a sufficiently traumatic incident/ period the original drivers may reassert themselves.]
Although not perfect, anyone attempting to move out of a Losing Script, may find a short period running a Boring Script can provide a much needed breathing space before attempting to create a Winning Script.

The term Sleepers is also taken from espionage where certain types of spy/ secret agent blend into the enemy country by being unassuming ordinary people. Never bringing suspicion upon themselves by doing something unusual or different.
 *See Glossary

*As with PAC; to keep this simple, scripts have been offered singularly as if we **only** run one script at a time; this being Winning, Boring or Losing. However we may adopt several different scripts in relationship to different spheres of existence. I.e. A Boring Script may be run at work, with a Losing Script reserved for marital relationships and a Winning Script for interests/ hobbies. Although under pressure we may revert to one habitual script. These mini-scripts are sometime referred to as plots.*

Hamartic/ Losing Scripts are unconscious or repressed. We often strive to achieve the opposite yet still succumb to the inevitable. Hamartic Scripts are less politely referred to as "Losing Scripts". Therefore people affected by and following Hamartic Scripts are often referred to as "Losers".

Losing Scripts are often compared to Greek tragedies. # One link is the hero with the fatal flaw i.e. Achilles.

It may be more appropriate to compare the scripts with TV Soap Operas; where we watch family, friends and neighbours; or even follow stories in the media where a tragedy unfolds. As with any Greek tragedy/ soap opera, the onlooker is well aware of the disaster the lead character is marching solidly towards, no matter what intervention is offered by onlookers or characters within the tragedy, the lead will continue marching towards his or her destruction. This causes additional horror or distress to the onlooker as we can see the lead character (friend, family or neighbour) heading towards self-destruction, whereas they do not perceive this.

Our character "appears" to be coping well even thriving, but at some point in the script their "fatal flaw" surfaces. As with Achilles they may appear unbeatable, yet just like Achilles, all they had to do was to protect the weak point. Armoured shoes/ boots would have saved Achilles but he didn't wear them. Our character is exactly the same. Whatever his or her fatal flaw is, they will leave it exposed until they lose and/ or die.

Originally compared to Greek tragedies by Claude M Steiner 1935- to date. (Scripts People Live – Grove Press. New York 2nd edition 1990).

It is an unfortunate aspect of a Losing Script that the person involved is nearly always oblivious to the impending doom, death or disaster they head towards. As with Greek tragedies, the lead character may be warned many times of the direction they are taking and the ultimate consequences they are facing, yet will forget, ignore, disregard etc. such sound advice and continue with their chosen script.

Losing Scripts are created and/ or heavily influenced by a significant adult [small a.] in the Child, usually (but not always) the mother or father.
The developing C/ child is directly affected by confused/ irrational adult in their own Child (victim*).
Scripts are supported/driven by "drivers". Drivers are created through observing the other significant adult; when coping with their partner.

Observations, of duty, loyalty etc. will create appropriate drivers in the developing Parent mind, as will anger and aggression, all of which will be used to "drive" the script in later life, i.e. a young child observes his mother as regularly hysterical, irrational, disturbed. His father usually puts up with this stoically, clinging to his (the father's) religious/ social/ moral values to continue in an irrational and unpleasant relationship.

Twenty years later, the young man falls in love with a bright/ beautiful/ exciting woman; ignoring her occasional irrational outbursts (*Everyone else notices these, but even brought to his attention, he will dismiss or ignore them*).
Shortly after the point of commitment* his partner changes. The irrational periods become more pronounced. Gradually, he will no longer feel loved/ happy. However, he will continue stoically with his relationship because *marriage is for life/ better or worse.* This particular person may stick rigidly to his marriage vows till death; or depression may set in where upon he may commit suicide. Either never knowing the script or realising perhaps too late that it was "predestined".
Sadly, if he survives the suicide attempt and/ or depression, but:-

i)   His marriage doesn't and/ or
ii)   He doesn't recognise the script

he will be attracted to a similar partner. Eventually repeating part of or the entire process again.
*See Glossary

Constrained by rules/ codes of honour, the "lead" in this example would be "driven" to remain with his partner until *she* left him. The idea of leaving would not be acceptable therefore the more he puts into the relationship, the greater the loss. Since the idea of leaving would not be acceptable, this would be one of the drivers in this particular relationship.

There is no need to suffer since as mentioned earlier, if the drivers are overcome the Script will collapse.

Another simplified example could be a young girl observing her father as regularly irrational/ aggressive (drunk?).

Her mother puts up with this stoically perhaps even attributing the blame for any physical assaults, to herself: - "I shouldn't have upset him when he is drunk", "I shouldn't have argued with him when he is angry/ upset".

Twenty years later this young lady falls in love with a bright/ handsome/ exciting man; ignoring his occasional angry moods. (Usually directed at someone/ thing else). *[Again, the audience: family, friends, etc. notice his behaviour, but she will dismiss their worries, as "he" loves her and would never hurt her!].*

True to form, shortly after the Point of Commitment* "he" changes; either becoming irrational and/ or getting drunk. Aggression/ violence may follow shortly thereafter.

Even though the lead in this situation may no longer feel loved (but may still love her partner), she continues stoically because "marriage is for life" or "you are married for better or worse". Depression may set in followed by suicide, or years of psychosomatic illness may ensue.

As with the previous example, if this woman survives any suicide attempts and/ or her depression, but: -

i)   her marriage doesn't and/ or

ii)   she doesn't recognise the script

she will continue repeating the process until partial or full recognition of the script ensues.
*See Glossary and relevant chapters.

92

This particular Script is further complicated where in her early childhood, lavish attention/ gifts etc. follow irrational moods/ actions by her father that were directed towards her. E.g. "Daddy didn't mean to frighten/ hurt his little princess. Come and have a cuddle. Now what could we do to make up; I know! We'll go to the beach/ park/ toy shop and give you a good time/ buy you a present."

Obviously, irrational behaviour and/ or negative strokes* are now connected to – associated with – love, affection, positive strokes, compensation.

Provided the previous example has this additional complication, the partner involved will regularly be '*forgiven*" on the condition that an appropriate level of love/ compensation ensues. This can be connected to a third degree Game# which may be played to the death (literally).

N.B. Partners that do not "perform" where the latter complication was discussed; may be "guided" (by their partner) until they learn and conform to the Script. I.e. a man with two to three previous relationships showing no sign of violence may at some stage after the Point of Commitment begin to lose his temper whereupon aggression/ drunkenness/ violence may occur. Filled with remorse he will act upon this providing suitable recompense. As such recompense usually matches the crime and that such recompense is seen unconsciously as evidence of love by his partner; then an escalation in frequency and/ or violence is only a matter of time. This and the previous examples occur in similar variations where gender is reversed and in homosexual relationships.

This does not mean that victims of domestic violence were "asking for it!" or that the perpetrator has no choice. But merely that where the Script is not recognised by either party, then the ability to exercise such choice is greatly reduced.

This book is not a manual to identify blame. It is a guide to observation, awareness, understanding, acceptance and hopefully subsequent change.

It should also be noted that the parents of the child in each example are likely to have suffered a similar process in their own childhood.

See Glossary and Chapter on Game Playing.

Types of Script

As mentioned earlier there are three different types of Script.
These are referred to as Winning, Banal and Hamartic; however, for the purpose of this book it will be easier to think of them as Winning, Boring and Losing, each of which could be first, second or third degree.

Winning Scripts

Winning Scripts are easy to identify; as the declared intent of the person running the Script is usually achieved i.e. the lead character declares that one-day they will be President/ Chief Exec of the company. Within a few short years and in extreme cases months, they actually become President/ Chief Exec of the company. Even *Losers* would recognise this as a Winning Script. However, the following example whilst clearly being a Winning Script might not be recognised as such by a *Loser*: -

The lead character declares that they don't want any responsibilities and don't want to work for a living. Sure enough within a short period of time they are unemployed and homeless, perhaps living as a gypsy or Hippy.

By a Loser's standards, this person is misperceived as a Loser because they have no money, no job, no home etc. But this is clearly a Winning Script because the lead character has achieved what they want. [In a *Losers* scenario this person would be declaring that all they want is a nice house and a steady job. At this point they would become a Loser!]

There is little point in labouring over Winning Scripts, since if you run them you needn't meddle with them. And if you don't run Winning Scripts, well they are pretty obvious as you achieve the things you set out to achieve. It is usually the Boring and Losing varieties that cause the most problems so most of this chapter is devoted to them.

It should be noted that whilst we adopt an overall Script for life, we also use a different mini-script [plot] for each area of our lives. We could have a Losing Script in our relationships, a Boring Script with our finances and a Winning Script at work. Depending on which one was second/ third degree would dictate the overall life Script. Or if you run three Losing mini-Scripts, one Boring mini-Script and one Winning mini-Script; you are running an overall Losing Script.

Boring Scripts

Boring Scripts should ideally be used as an intermediary period between a Winning and a Losing Script or a Losing Script and a Winning Script.

This gives the impression that there is some conscious awareness or choice when someone running a Winning Script changes to a Losing Script.

[The obvious question is why on earth would a *winner* **choose** to be a *loser*? Remember Scripts are created in those early years of life in the unconscious mind without any rational thought from the conscious Adult mind. The unconscious mind uses a different form of logic to the conscious mind, having it's own reasons for losing instead of winning.]

But this is not the case. It appears that adopting a Boring Script on the way down is a survival mechanism used by the unconscious mind to limit the damage. The converse is also true. Since changing *Losers* rarely have a conscious awareness that they are en-route to Winning. The unconscious mind adopts a Boring Script to create a stable platform (or a series of stable platforms) so that the lead character can step up to a Winning Script.

It is assumed that Boring Scripts should be temporary and a suggested maximum period that a Boring Script should be run for is two to three years. With an ideal period of six months, being enough time to stabilise things before moving on.

Unfortunately, some people adopt a Boring Script for life.

Whilst this is understandable, since these people would not have any particularly painful or serious ups or downs in their life, it is not an acceptable way to enjoy life. These particular characters convince themselves that they are enjoying life but they are in fact existing, although by *Losers* standards they are existing comfortably.

Many people that run a Boring Script for life are the basest of animals. A pig exists from the day it's born to the day it dies, rooting around, sleeping, eating, copulating, farting, etc. **because** it has no other choice! Other mammals do not have rational thought of, nor do they evidence an Adult mind. Humans do! To live a Banal existence when there is an alternative choice denies all that we are; **unless you are truly and blissfully happy**. Most people that run Boring Scripts are not.

If you are truly and blissfully happy [as opposed to most people that confuse lack of unhappiness, with happiness. They are two quite different states.] then by default you are running a Winning Script, since people running Winning Scripts achieve what they want.

In poll after poll, survey after survey people consistently put being happy as their number one desire.

An example of a life long Boring Script would be someone who works 47 years to his or her retirement in the same or similar job and retires as the team leader or junior manager. This person is quite unaware that their entire achievement in their career is to move one or perhaps two rungs up the ladder, something they have taken 47 years to achieve that most people could achieve in four to five years.

Again, as with any other script they will convince themselves and the people around them that they are right. Perhaps they are? After all, at retirement this person will have almost certainly paid their mortgage off, probably buys a new car every two or three years, has a modest but safe sum of money invested and probably has remained with the same partner for many years. Their entire life has become repetitive and predictable, although again these characters will carry out actions that they mistakenly believe are unpredictable.

Their Boring Script may be so extreme that they have the same meal every day of the week. I.e. Monday night is pizza night, Tuesday night is meat loaf night, etc. (The particularly sad thing is that they probably have the **same** type of pizza every Monday; if they started at the beginning of their career they will have had almost 2,500 identical pizzas by the time they retire!)

Occasionally, they may do something incredibly daring and right out of the blue declare that tonight they will go out for a meal or order a take-away. Obviously, they will either go to the same or a similar restaurant and order their usual. They will also be unaware that their random and *unpredictable* action occurs about once a month; so although it appears random there is a pattern.

Boring Scripts are similar to and work in conjunction with the Parent mind. Basically, they get things done. Life becomes easier.

If you know what meals are going to be eaten each day of the week, then your shopping becomes easier and again identical. Every weekly shop you will purchase exactly the same items as you purchased last week. Shopping now becomes quicker and easier to budget for. However, just to convince yourself that you couldn't **possibly be boring,** you buy an unusual treat/ desert although as mentioned earlier this is something you do regularly, i.e. once a month.

We are now changing evolution from the survival of the fittest to the survival of the thickest [mentally]. We are becoming a species of nit-picking inferior creatures, where second rate is safer and therefore more valuable than first rate.

It isn't that long ago people wanted to become discoverers, explorers, inventors, pioneers, writers, etc. i.e. They were prepared to give up part of their lives [perhaps even prepared to die in the attempt] to provide something better for humanity and society.

Now people choose to become owners, to have material possessions. I.e. they merely wish to take from humanity and society. Of course they give lip-service to ideas of ecology/ limited resources/ global warming/ etc. whilst still demanding Brand name goods, bigger and better cars, new fashions every season, etc.

In fact one well known "green" cosmetics and gifts company, push the ecologically sound nature of their products whilst encouraging people to buy more and more soaps, bath oils, shampoo, etc.; plus (of course) all sorts of fancy packaging [usually consisting of four sheets of coloured cellophane, eighteen rolled up sheets of coloured tissue paper, three ribbons, various pieces of straw/ plastic/ wood/ etc. and a very pretty (but quite useless) woven basket] is used. Not surprisingly this is sound and very profitable business sense. The Child mind wants to buy pretty and fancily wrapped goods, even if they are not needed or necessary.

Well I don't know about you but this certainly doesn't sound very "green" to me!

Losing Scripts

The commonest scripts that people run are Losing Scripts.

As a general rule a *loser* declares certain aims/ wants in life but rarely if ever attains them.

He or she may work incredibly hard at whatever it is they wish, or they may do nothing at all. However this is played they will still lose!

The severity of losing usually depends on the degree that the Script is being played/ followed. As such this particular section will be described within the degrees that it can be played. [NB All types of Script can be played/ followed in three degrees.]

There are three degrees to a Losing Script.

In a first degree Losing Script, the lead character's actions and behaviour are usually just a nuisance. This is due to first degree Scripters following the Script like young children in the school play: -

> sometimes excited, sometimes bored, occasionally forgetting their lines, losing the direction, etc. One minute they are "in Script" the next they aren't.

In a second degree Losing Script, the lead character's actions and behaviours have a direct affect on the people around them often drawing them into the Script as additional characters. This may cause partners, family and friends running boring Scripts to be drawn into Losing Scripts and is therefore much more than a nuisance. People running second degree Scripts are similar to people involved in amateur dramatics: -

> becoming keener as the rehearsals progress, often competent, occasional delays, occasionally outstanding, sometimes slow to start becoming dedicated as the play progresses, etc.

In a third degree Losing Script, the lead character is often destroyed. In real terms this usually means Court appearances/ prison, serious injuries and/or death. Sadly, a third degree character will often drag their partners, families and friends into second-degree Scripts themselves.

Third degree Scripters follow the Script as seasoned professionals:-

> rehearsing so intently that they become the characters involved i.e. "in character", give total commitment, are totally plausible, will continue regardless of interruptions or audience participation, etc. Will follow the Script to its bitter end, even "to the death!".

To recap: - as with Game Playing, the level or intensity with which a Script is adhered to varies with three levels. As a rough guide, level one (first degree) Script is merely a nuisance. The person running a Losing (first degree) Script wishes to be promoted at work perhaps eventually to be a director yet regularly arrives ten minutes late for work. This is enough to be noticed (but not enough to be dismissed), therefore holding this person back from a promotion occasionally.

Again, roughly, a level two (second-degree) Script is more intrusive.
Using the above example, this character in the second degree Script regularly misses deadlines, wastes company money/ time and causes enough trouble to be demoted, perhaps even dismissed. Yet still professes an earnest desire for promotion.

And finally, a rough guide to level three (third degree). The same scenario running a third degree Losing Script, our character may actually be stealing company money/ secrets/ equipment, they may get disillusioned over many years and might actually attack their immediate manager; this may occur at/ or through their annual appraisal/ assessment. These actions may lead to prison or even death. Third degree Scripts and third degree Game Playing, are played "for keeps". The result is usually irreversible.

The distinction drawn between first, second and third degrees are arbitrary since one person's first degree could be another's second and vice-versa. The distinctions drawn in these examples are used to aid understanding but are not necessarily fixed positions in someone's life.
Depending on their partners' Script/s, running a first degree losing Script involving gambling may be quite sufficient to cause divorce. This is obviously more than a nuisance and therefore this particular couple would be considered second or even third degree rather than first. If the partner's Parent mind has no particular objection to modest gambling then the lead character's behaviour is merely a nuisance and will be assessed as first degree.

An example of these is someone that regularly proclaims that one-day they are going to be a millionaire/ win the lottery. They then usually put their life on hold until they have sufficient money i.e. First degree "when I win the lottery, I going to have/ do/ buy/ etc.". Second degree "when I win the lottery, <u>we</u> will/ can/ etc." Therefore involving their partners and/ or family.

Although the declared intent is to have sufficient funds at some point in their life to carry out whatever it is they wish to do, our losing Scripter will actually do the opposite.

In a first degree Script, this particular lead character (assuming 20k £/$ income per annum) will be spending approximately 20 to 40 £/$ per week in bets (including the lottery). Clearly, this is **just** a nuisance, obviously it will be nice to keep this money in the family budget, but it won't particularly damage the family standards. This may go on for many years with little gaps when the lead character isn't *pushed* into their Script.

In a second degree Script, this particular lead character (again assuming 20k £/$ income per annum) may now be spending 80 to 120 £/$ per week in bets. This is no longer just a nuisance as every member of this person's immediate family is being affected. This clearly intrudes upon family life. Holidays are cancelled, parties are cancelled, and even the type of food the family eats has changed. The partner <u>must</u> find savings in the family's finances, cans of value baked beans at a few cents/ pennies are no longer an option but are now a necessity.

The longer this person adopts a second degree Script, the heavier the penalty paid by their partner and children. At some point their children's clothes will now be being bought at Charity shops. Soon all of the family's clothes are being purchased at Charity shops. Children may do without; pressure builds up in the family, which may lead to divorce and/ or hardship. Debt is starting to become a constant companion.

Eventually, this will spiral into a third degree.

In a third degree Script, this particular lead character (again assuming 20k £/$ income per annum) may now be spending 160 to 240 £/$ per week, clearly the income does not support this expenditure. Bills aren't being paid, large debts may be being run up. I.e. the house may be re-mortgaged and serious bank loans may be outstanding.

In some horrifying situations their partner is quite unaware of these facts and believes whatever tale the lead character has told them. They are likely to have run out of legitimate sources to borrow money from. It is possible at this stage that if their work allows it (i.e. Accounts/ banking/ finance) they may begin to steal money [often with the pseudo-legitimate excuse that they are really just *borrowing* the money and that they fully intend to pay it back one day!] from their company. Or they may go to a loan shark.

If they steal money, it is only a matter of time before they are dismissed and/ or end up in prison. If they borrow from a loan shark, it is only a matter of time before their partner or children have their legs broken.
Contrary to Hollywood fiction, it is not the person who reneges on the loan that will initially have their legs broken. The type of loan shark we are discussing will realise that certain types of *loser* will accept two broken legs as a reasonable price to pay for failing to return a £/$50,000 loan. Although **you** may find this peculiar, to a *loser* on 20k £/$ per annum, six months in plaster for £/$50,000 loan if it can be repeated puts their annual income up to £/$100,000.

[With a *losing* Script they couldn't possibly earn this.]#

Therefore the loan shark's only choice is to put pressure on through the family members and if this fails, to kill the lead character. After all, if they (the loan shark) have 2 to 3 million £/$ loaned to various *losers* they stand to lose everything if those *losers* believe they can get away with not paying it back.

If just one *loser* gets away without paying, all of the other *losers* will believe they can to.

#With a Winning Script **anyone** regardless of their IQ, qualifications, background, social status, etc. if they truly intended/ wanted to, **can** earn this level of income.

Scripts are supported/ fed by "drivers"; therefore the intensity of the degree equates directly to the intensity of the driver. In the example given above, on a first-degree script the driver may be "somebody has to win the lottery, why shouldn't it be me?" or "If you're not in it, you can't win it!". In this case it is just the phrases/ words that **drive** you.

On a second degree Script the drivers may be "I've been losing money for so long, the odds must be in my favour, therefore I'll win as long as I keep betting. However to get back the money I've lost I have to put on bigger bets!"; usually now picking horses/ dogs with outlandish odds, losing big time.

Or you win £/$1,500 in a multiple bet, and are now sure you know how to and/ or can beat the system. You spend £/$25,000 over the next five years trying to win £/$1,500 again. In this case the driver is the *belief* and the *emotions* connected to it, that **drives** you on.

Similar drivers are used in the third degree Script. The actual amounts are just increased. I.e. you win £/$15,000 but you spend £/$250,000 over five to ten years trying to repeat the big win.

It is important to understand with drivers that they are based on **feelings** and not rational thought. The character in all three examples of degrees *knows* that the driver is valid. They can *feel* it in their bones.

Usually first degree *hope* they'll win, second degree *feel* they can win, third degree *know* they'll win. They don't of course, but still stick to their scripts.

This may be the reason why they have retained and followed their drivers even though friends and family have pointed out how irrational that driver may be. Whilst using a third degree driver, someone points out that spending tens of thousands, then hundreds of thousands in an attempt to repeat a £/$15,000 win is irrational. On hearing this, you merely adopt the earlier driver, that you have lost that many bets that it is only a matter of time before you hit the big win again. I.e. The odds are with you.

Unfortunately the horses that you bet on that day are unaware of your string of losses. As such they won't make the slightest effort to pass the finish line in your favour!

Whilst Scripts have been mentioned singularly and from the viewpoint of the individual; Scripts can be sociological in that families, groups, cultures, and possibly entire countries follow Scripts. Usually where a culture runs a Script, there is a recognisable uniform and "sets" so that we can recognise the Scripters.

You wouldn't be surprised to see longhaired, tattoo covered, leather clad people at a "Biker Bar". You might expect these people to be *"losers"*, perhaps connected to drugs, alcohol abuse and violence; almost certainly just one arrest away from prison. You probably wouldn't expect these people to be involved in charity work (unless it is to help themselves!).

Yet with *my* local bike groups, regular days are allocated as "pet food" runs to the local animal shelters and "toy runs" to the local hospitals.

It doesn't seem right does it? Picture it in your mind now. Several hundred motor cycles rolling by in a blue/ brown haze of exhaust fumes and dust, in an archetypal true Harley-Davidson™ style of "Rolling Thunder". Everyone happy, shouting above the noise, cheerful, always a sense of purpose and direction, bonding in a positive way, with an overwhelming feeling of camaraderie.

If anyone breaks down, several other bikers will stop to help, not necessarily because they know the person who has broken down, but purely because they are bikers. I.e. members of an international club, merely by being on two wheels since all bikers face the same dangers* and recognise that anyone else on two wheels is truly a brother/ sister in arms.

Clearly, whether these particular bikers are on an overall Losing Script or not; on that particular day every one of them is and far more importantly, feels that they are running a Winning Script.

For a short period, regardless of colour, creed, gender, age, etc. **everyone** is truly accepted just because they are bikers. (Although they are often referred to as bikers for being on two wheels; this also includes trikes.)

*Usually from "Cagers" [see Glossary], civic offices failing to maintain public highways to a standard safe for *two-wheeled* use, utility companies using cheap/ inappropriate surfacing when laying/ repairing lines/ pipes/ etc., diesel users, weather conditions, etc.

Although in a similar manner to George Orwell's Animal Farm, some are more equal than others. But the differences are usually used for good-hearted banter, since some bikes are literally home made, some may be "Harley-Davidson's" or "Harley clones" and some may be plastic road-rockets. The choice of motorcycle and relevant modifications is a reflection of the Biker [and their finances] at that point in their lives.

Regardless of the motor cycle, every biker takes the same risks!

Also whilst each person's contribution is in itself negligible, as a **group** we truly make a difference.

Perhaps you could argue that we do it to see the look of appreciation in the animals' eyes at the shelters, but using your Adult mind you would realise that the stray dogs and cats aren't actually aware that we have delivered food and/ or that it is for them.

The simple truth is that we do it for **ourselves** and for the pleasure that comes from these actions.

Perhaps for some [certainly for myself], the recognition that no matter how small we really **can** make a difference.

This is truly the behaviour of winners.

Strangely enough this behaviour affects others since when the Toy runs are organised, many local companies [and in particular independent traders] donate Toys, even though they are not actually on the *run*; understanding that the children will not actually know who donated what?

Again it is not the recognition that is important but the actions.

"…. Several hundred motorcycles rolling by in a blue/ brown haze of exhaust fumes and dust, in an archetypal true Harley-Davidson™ style of "Rolling Thunder". Everyone happy, shouting above the noise, cheerful, always a sense of purpose and direction, bonding in a positive way, with an overwhelming feeling of camaraderie… This is truly the behaviour of winners.

This particular illustration represents **the feeling of freedom** biking gives. For many riders, biking is a lifestyle, a way of living.

The illustration is drawn American style [note the lack of crash helmet; for those of you that may be interested: Scientists/ academics "proved" that wearing crash helmets would save lives. Several American States promptly legislated for the compulsory wearing of crash helmets. When **real** statistics (i.e. What **actually** happened, rather than the predicted statistics used by the scientists!) revealed that the number of motorcycle accidents (and deaths) **increased** when Bikers wore crash helmets; that legislation [in some states] was repealed. Yet in the UK it is still compulsory to wear a crash helmet. Strange isn't it?   I'm allowed to smoke unlimited cigarettes and get lung cancer, drink unlimited amounts of alcohol perhaps dying from cirrhosis of the liver, have unsafe sex, have mercury fillings in my teeth, take unlimited amounts of aspirin/ ibuprofen, etc., ride a horse without any form of safety gear, have a boxing match. But I will be sent to jail if I ride a motorcycle without a helmet!

Practise

As with any competent thespian, we practise/ rehearse our lines, actions and gestures until we are word perfect. As we get closer to the first night, we begin to dress according to our role; our transport, our jobs; our partners, friends etc. are all chosen specifically to make our Script plausible. Like the seasoned thespians we become; we live, eat and breathe our Scripts until we are *that* character, whether our character is a hero/ine, clown, villain, *persecutor, rescuer*, and *victim** etc.

This process begins from the moment we have decided upon our life Script. Even at four or five years of age we are beginning to practise the words, phrases and gestures that will eventually lead to total plausibility.

The moment we can get away with it #, we will begin to adopt friends and colleagues that will support our particular Script; sometimes this begins at school and college, sometimes we wait until we are adults.

We also begin to choose cultural actions that allow us to be recognised as the lead character in our own particular life Script. I.e. Our chosen life Script is a losing Script, perhaps entitled "What's the Point?". At school we gravitate towards other "losers" perhaps joining the smoking/ gambling club in the toilets/ changing rooms. We begin to skip lessons. Long ago we gave up on homework, deciding that we would never make the grade so *what's the point*? We become interested in the clothes and attitudes of our fellow club members, perhaps even already beginning to look like young "down and outs" or thugs.

When we are invited to leave school (perhaps through being expelled or enjoying a short stay at a Young Offender's Institute), we either try for State Benefits or perhaps for a very short period try a dead-end job before once again we think *what's the point?*

#We rarely receive parental permission to act like a loser. However, we may receive parental support if acting like a winner.

* See Glossary.

It is only a matter of time before we gravitate towards excess alcohol and/ or street drugs. The great beauty about Marijuana is it is the perfect *what the heck/ what's the point?* drug. Over a period of time and with regular use Marijuana de-motivates, and to be fair if you wish to remain unemployed/ loser, then it should be something that you could legally use. After all, at some point in their life most losers will eventually find things become pretty shitty - therefore a chance to switch off and forget about things/ to chill out at a reasonable financial price should be an option.

The problem with street drugs is that they are illegal; as a loser it won't be too long before your *what's the point?* attitude, drives you to the belief that since you are already breaking the law with your habits, it hardly matters if you break the law further to maintain those habits.

In true chronic second degree losing style you gradually gravitate towards third degree and prison or death perhaps through substance abuse or violence. I.e. the final scene has arrived.

OR

You are running a Winning Script perhaps entitled "No Problem".

At school you find that you gravitate towards the more successful students. Although we will be using "The Nerd" route as an example, it could just as easily been "The Jock" route. You find that by a modest amount of effort you begin to pick up academic information quite easily. Your grades improve and you get into a routine with your homework. Extra work, projects, extra curriculum assignments all get created quite positively with either the thought or the phrase "no problem".

You work your way through College/ University without too much difficulty, and gain a fairly good foothold in the company/ industry of your choice.

Perhaps without even realising it you are now on the fast track.

No matter what the task or difficulty at work you greet it all with the unconscious belief that it's *no problem*. This is likely to gain you a reputation as an achiever/ problem solver; it is only a matter of time before you come to the Chief Exec/ Managing Director's attention.

Directorship or Vice Presidency is now in the pipeline.

Long before you reach this stage you will have adopted the language, gestures, interests and even the clothes of a successful person. *You* didn't have to go to seminars or workshops to teach you, that you should always dress for the post above your present position. Since, because you run a Winning Script, this came naturally. [It is only "losers" that need to be *trained* to become winners; unfortunately as true "losers" they will forget, disregard, or ignore all that useful information. So they will need another course!].

You will gravitate towards successful people unconsciously picking up their skills, behaviour, gestures and language until you are the successful person that other *winners* now gravitate towards.

Script names

Transactional Analysis is riddled with nicknames and in-house phrases.

Where appropriate these have been filtered out to allow a better understanding of TA. Occasionally, new nicknames have been put in i.e. replacing Banal with Boring, Hamartic with Losing, making Scripts much more understandable.

The following nickname can be used for both the lead character and the Losing Script. Certain forms of Losing Scripts may be referred to as "Fatal Flaw Scripts".

A Fatal Flaw Script is a direct reference to the hero Achilles. According to history/ legend, Achilles was invincible therefore the few pictures that represent Achilles wearing a helmet and breast plate seem peculiar since Achilles could not be harmed. His fatal flaw was his heel, which was the only part of his body that could be punctured by sword, spear or arrow. This eventually lead to his death when a poisoned arrow struck his heel.

Achilles representing the Fatal Flaw Script. Frank's been at it again since the shield has three faces/ minds. Do we use our minds as a shield? In the past the shield was often also used as a weapon, do we use our minds as weapons? How much unnecessary "armour" do you carry? If you have one, what is your fatal flaw?

The idea of a fatal flaw becomes more understandable with the realisation that Achilles **knew** this part of his body was vulnerable; therefore the **only** part of his body he needed to protect with armour was his heel. By leaving his heel uncovered, he was running a Losing Script even though he acted like a winner. He was tempting fate and lost. This is a neat example of a third degree Losing Script since this fatal flaw led directly to Achilles' death.

It is a common theme of some Losing Scripts that the lead character will have some kind of fatal flaw. Regardless of their apparent good intent or actions that may appear to be connected to winning; their fatal flaw will ultimately lead to their demise. Occasionally, like Achilles the fatal flaw might be physical but usually it is psychological. The fatal flaw will be a hidden psychological/ emotional virus that will surface at the point that the lead character appears invincible and/ or just short of winning.

Like Achilles, this will have been something that the lead character was aware of in their dim and distant past but either forgotten or ignored. It is also likely that this is something the lead character should have protected but didn't. I.e. you have done reasonably well at college but haven't decided your direction in life yet. So you sign up for a short period of military service. After a couple of years you begin to realise that you have an alcohol problem.

On completing your military service you discover that leaving the pressure and the environment your alcohol problem settles down.

Some time later (10-15-20 years), you are one step away from senior management. Although your rise has been steady rather than meteoric, you have been invincible. This final step is proven success. There is just the pressure of your last presentation to the Board. As the pressure builds up, you have a drink so you can relax/ unwind/ sleep at night. As the pressure continues to build up, one drink is no longer enough.

Since you are running a losing Script, if at a first-degree level, your drinking habits will usually cost you your promotion (and any chance of senior management). If it is really light first degree you may be offered the opportunity to "dry out" and if things are fine in six months time be offered the post again.

If at a second-degree level, your drinking habits will affect your job at your present level, perhaps leading to demotion or even dismissal (if you are incredibly lucky, early retirement).

If it is third degree, your drinking habits may lead to complete collapse of both your work, social, financial and domestic life. (Probably involving a Court appearance and perhaps even suicide).

Ironically we adopt our Script in our third or fourth year of life through observation of our parents, which then means our ultimate demise or success which is predestined in our adult life, may actually have been unconsciously dictated by our parents before we were even born.

We may merely be the second or third degree of our parents Script!

Since this book relies heavily on common sense I am not suggesting that we are all genetically predisposed to misery, doom and destruction.

Rather that the script itself may be predestined or *seeded* before we are born.

To make things worse the very name that our parents choose for us, could also predestine our Script.

Names are often chosen from a relative, a biblical character, a fairy tale character, a television character, a historical figure and may be indicative of a hero/ ine, villain, leader, fool, tragic clown etc. This has a profound effect on the development of the child.

By thinking of some names this will all become very obvious.

Telling a young girl that she is named Florence after Florence Nightingale will give a considerably different Script message to telling her that she is named Florence after the city (Italy) or Florence from the Magic Roundabout. Or perhaps interpreting the name as the essence of flowers.

Similarly, what kind of Script message do you think you are giving your daughter in connection to long life, family harmony and marital happiness if you call her Juliet?

In the latter example, the more this young lady understands the story of Romeo and Juliet the more her unconscious mind will reinforce a losing Script in connection to long life and marital happiness. Perhaps more importantly (from your point of view) she may now be predestined to fall in love with the son of your greatest enemy.

Remember that *third degree Scripts* end in death and/ or court, usually prison. Since Romeo and Juliet is a tragedy you may have inadvertently not only given your daughter a Losing Script, but ultimately a third degree Losing Script.

Similarly you would hardly expect your son to grow up with good social skills and a wide range of true and trusted friends if you chose to name him Judas.

At this stage you may mistakenly believe that things would be much safer if you named your child after a relative. You couldn't be further from the truth. Grandma/ dad may be delighted that their grandchild is named after them but they lived in a different era with different attitudes and values of life.

Not all old-fashioned values are suitable for modern life. In addition, the grandparent would either have been affected themselves by their name or be running a Script.

Naturally, the child will adopt their namesake's attitudes, gestures, language and Script.

However, just in case the child by some miracle manages to avoid being drawn into this, their entire family will put them back on to the right path. Usually with comments such as s/ he has Grandma/ dad's: - temper/ musical ability/ appetite/ sense of humour/ intelligence/ accident proneness/ etc.

Naturally, the child will adopt and practice these *skills* ready for the big day (the opening night of their particular play/ life Script).

Even apparently innocent names can have a profound effect on a child since there are many books on the interpretation of and hidden meaning of names.

Even our **birth date** can have a profound effect on our Script.

Since many people find it far too tempting to look up "their stars" often believing implicitly that since they are "a fire/ water/ earth/ air sign", the listed character traits listed for that sign are theirs.

Even when the interpretation is absolutely ludicrous they will still believe part of, if not all of the predictions for their star sign that day.

Great Britain has a population of approximately 60 million people. Since there are twelve star signs, a rough average would give 5 million people per prediction. It hardly takes a genius to realise that with 5 million people representing each sign in just one country, that the most outlandish prediction will have at least one person enact it.

For example, in true astrological style I hereby predict that in the coming year Sagittarians will be both lucky and unlucky, that romance may be on the horizon and that there will be upheaval on the domestic front.

In fact, I will even be quite specific. This week a Sagittarian will win the lottery (although I haven't said how much) and there will be upheaval in their work life (although again I haven't said exactly what).

Obviously this is ridiculous, because with 5 million Sagittarians in the UK, of course one of them will win the lottery.

In fact, if a financial amount is not specified, then approximately 200,000 Sagittarians will win the lottery this. Due to the law of averages most of these will have the lowest prize but it is also possible that one of them will win the top prize.

The same rules apply to the prediction of upheaval at work. Most of our "lottery winning" Sagittarians will notice some kind of minor change during the week at work; therefore the entire prediction becomes true.

As with the lottery prediction, a significant number perhaps 200,000 to 300,000 will have a fairly serious upheaval at work. These will include promotions, demotions, hiring and firing. Also just because of the number of fires, accidents and burglaries in a week; a noticeable number perhaps 1,000 or 2,000 will have a very serious upheaval at work.

If I was an astrologer, gaining a dozen outstanding testimonials from Sagittarians that had substantial wins on the lottery and had noticeable upheaval at work, would hardly be difficult!

Purely because of the laws of averages the same prediction in the same week will be valid for _every_ star sign. Honestly! Work it out for yourself.

Even when using your Adult mind you understand and accept the above premise, if your particular Child or Parent mind believes in astrology, you will still find yourself looking up your horoscope.
Since *adults* have difficulty overriding their Child or Parent with reasoning, a young child without a functioning Adult mind won't stand a chance. Therefore adopting whatever attributes or skills their star sign awards them.

Now start adding cultural, religious, ancestral history to this equation and you can begin to see how easy it is for a young child to be predestined to win or fail.

Regardless of their circumstances a child can "inherit" a Script, regardless of their potential inherited Script, a child's circumstances can craft a new/ alternative Script. It depends on the child and their parents.

*Also as Adults, with knowledge and purpose **all** Scripts can be re-written.*

Script Names

There are many variations of the three main themes in Scripts, each having their own name. Some Scripts are a mixture of themes such as partial winner and partial boring. Some common mixtures have specific titles such as the "Fatal Flaw Script", being a mixture of winning and ultimately losing Script.

The names of individual Scripts have been left out of this book in order to simplify this chapter, since there are potentially more names of Scripts than there are plays and films. However it can be fun to recognise a Script and give it your own personal name: -

an "Aunt Betty",

Or if you prefer working in-groups, a name the group can identify with: -

A "Hamlet", or a "Joan of Arc", or a "Homer Simpson" or whatever.

There are no hard rules for naming Scripts, just go with whatever works for you.

Although as general rule, the more fun [go on be naughty, use "gleeful vindictiveness. I.e. those kinds of thoughts and words that are quite near the knuckle. You'd hardly tell this person their nickname, would you? This is just your private fun to help you to learn to recognise Scripty behaviour.] you have with the names the easier it will be to recognise Script behaviour.

Recognising Script behaviour in oneself is a first step in altering it to your preferred Script. However your unconscious mind truly believes that when you are under pressure/ stress your personal Script/ s will save you; as such they are devious beasts and will resurrect themselves in the most innovative manner. Do not be disheartened, modifying the drivers of a Script will eventually change it.

In fact just **recognising** a first degree Script can be enough to get it under control.

Counter Scripts

Counter Scripts are traditionally taught by psychologists, counsellors, therapists, etc. enabling their clients/ patients to move away from losing Scripts and/ or destructive behaviour.

Although this appears simple it usually requires a third party such as a therapist to identify a suitable counter Script.

To create a counter Script, identify a Script used by a winner, a hero/ine, a historical figure, etc. that you wish to have. Locate the relevant Drivers, then use those Drivers <u>consistently</u> and <u>relentlessly</u>.

However it is essential that one of the major drivers and/ or several of the minor drivers in the old Script have been discounted, before creating a counter Script.

Drivers can be discounted by assessing them with the Adult mind, applying logic and accepting the result.

E.g. In the gambling scenario one of the drivers is a belief that having lost X amount of money betting on horses, the odds are that you must win soon. In applying the Adult mind it can be accepted that the horses involved in your next bet have no awareness of these odds. Even if they were capable of knowing, it is unlikely that the one you bet on can run any faster this time than it would have anyway!

P.P.P.'s

- Scripts originate in early childhood.

- Created through both direct observation and instructions from parents: - " if our Joey doesn't get his act together, he'll never amount to anything" or "if you don't behave you'll grow up to be a loser, just like your father!".

- Three types: - Winning, Boring [Banal], and Losing [Hamartic].

- Winning Scripters usually achieve their desired goals/ aims. Often referred to as "Winners".

- Boring Scripters usually make their lives easy by not "rocking the boat". Often referred to as "Sleepers" and more cruelly especially in third degree as "Zombies".

- Losing Scripters usually fail to achieve their desired goals/ aims. An exception being Fatal Flaw Scripters who temporarily appear to win/ achieve their desires, but will if continuing in Script ultimately lose. Often referred to as "Losers" or "Marvins" [after Marvin the depressed robot in "The Hitch Hikers Guide to the Galaxy", Douglas Adams.]

- There are three degrees of Scripting: First, second and third.

- First degree Scripters follow the Script like young children in a school play: - sometimes excited, sometimes are bored, occasionally forgetting their lines, etc.

- Second degree Scripters follow the script like amateur dramatics: - quite keen, reasonable rehearsals, often competent, occasionally outstanding, etc.

- Counter Script is a mechanism that can over-ride an inappropriate Script. Usually but not always: a Boring Script is the Counter Script for a Losing Script, a Winning Script is a Counter Script for a Boring Script. However in second and third degree Losing Scripts, sometimes a first degree Losing Script will be used as the first Counter Script, before moving into a Boring Script.

117

- Third degree Scripters follow the Script as seasoned professionals: - intense rehearsals, totally plausible, totally committed, totally "in character", etc.

- Fatal Flaw Script/ Achilles Heel Script is a specific type of losing Script usually third degree. It mimics a Winning Script until the point where success is almost inevitable, then with considerable style one action/ event turns the win into a loss.

- All Scripts are supported by "drivers".

- Drivers can be emotional, physiological [adrenaline & nor-adrenaline], and phrases.

- Physiological and emotional drivers can de-commission the Adult mind. Usually the greater the intensity the more complete the de-commissioning.

- Phrases are usually pseudo-legitimate excuses or *rules* in the Parent and Child minds.

- Generally a Script is supported by two or three *global* drivers and/ or dozens of *local* drivers. E.g. Local driver: - I've picked 1, 7, 8, & 12 as my lottery numbers; because 1 is my lucky number, 7 & 8 because it's the 7th August, my niece is 12 this year, etc. Global drivers: - I've got to win soon since I've put £/$12,000 on the lottery in the past year.

- Local Drivers are usually unique to the Scripter, although they often come from common sources.

- Many people have a *lucky* pen/ key ring/ money clip/ purse/ rabbits foot/ talisman/ etc. technically these are both Global and Local. Since it is common for people to have something that is *lucky,* but unique in that the chosen object is usually personal in some way to the owner.

- Global Drivers are usually common to that type of Script. I.e. Many gamblers running losing Scripts really do believe "that their luck must change soon", or that because they have lost X amount of money/ times they must win soon.

STAMP COLLECTING

Stamp Collecting is almost an extension of Strokes; since positive, negative and plastic Strokes are collected as Stamps.

Stamp Collecting was originally compared to the collecting of "trading stamps" which at some point would be redeemed for goods/ merchandise.*

However, I prefer to compare Stamp Collecting with philately where enthusiasts and beginners alike all collect different sizes, values and intensities of coloured stamps. Each stamp collector has their favourite or preferred type of stamp. Some collectors will only collect stamps of one nation or one theme i.e. wildlife, or one period i.e. 1905-1935.

Psychological Stamp Collectors are very similar although we may collect any stamp, we often have a preferred type i.e. fear stamps, stupid stamps, guilt stamps, envy stamps, anger stamps etc. And just like philately there are all sorts of different sizes and intensities of each of these stamps. The intensity/ size is directly equal to the value of strokes gained, lost or owed.

☐ ☐ ☐   = 3 strokes

☐   = 25 strokes

*Winning with People, Jongeward and James, 1973 Addison-Wesley Publishing Company.

We probably keep a different stamp book for different areas/ Scripts in our life. Perhaps work produces five or six new "one Stroke stamps" each day. Eventually these will build up until a considerable amount of the stamp book is filled. At this point we may attempt to trade them in for promotion or pay rise. Assuming we are successful the book is cleared or closed and we begin a new one. If we get the pay rise we are expecting we start a new book perhaps keeping one or two favourite stamps.

However, if we are passed over for promotion or pay rise, we feel cheated and may want the value of all the stamps back at once.

We may even resign feeling bitter or perhaps take the company to court on charges of sexual discrimination/ racial discrimination/ constructive dismissal etc. (This is not to suggest that all cases of sexual/ racial discrimination/ constructive dismissal etc. are merely acts of vindictiveness due to a subjective perception over what the company owes.)

Please read this it is important: -

Stamp collecting is subjective in that the "Company" has little or no idea that <u>you</u> kept a stamp collection. You and you alone decide the value of each stamp. Every stamp represents an action or an effort on your behalf that you feel was carried out for the company **above and beyond** your contracted work.

Every favour for a boss or work colleague may become a stamp that the "Company" now owes you.

It is likely that the Company attitude is probably along the lines that you get a salary and benefits therefore they own you for that period, therefore you are not entitled to any further consideration. It is also possible that as your stamp book fills you become jaded and your quality of work suffers accordingly. If this has occurred and you have ten years of outstanding "favour stamps" then you will expect the next promotion. But a whiz kid with only six months experience but producing a higher quality/ quantity of work and only having six months of favour stamps is more likely to receive the promotion.

Whilst it is easy to understand your point of view and your frustration/ unhappiness; it is important to understand that companies are often unaware of favours given to individual bosses. If that boss is not directly responsible for, or has the ability to promote you then you are in the hands of someone else (i.e. Personnel), who has no idea that the Company "owes you", therefore cannot take this into account.

Even if companies did take stamp collecting into account when it came to promotions and pay rises, people would still be unhappy because the company assessor may have a completely different idea of the value of your stamps.

[This is one of the reasons why I like to compare this process with philately. It is not usual for someone to carefully collect a specific type of stamp filling album after album becoming more and more excited by each (as far as they are concerned) rare addition. Years later when their interest fades and/or they need some money, they may take the collection to a dealer who promptly offers them fifty percent less than the actual cost of purchasing the stamps in the first place whereas you were expecting three or four hundred percent more. The dealer is not necessarily trying to rip you off as they are offering you a rate in comparison to **their** view of the present value of your collection.]

Personnel departments in companies would be similar in that their idea of the value of each favour/ additional effort that you have put into the company may be considerably lower than you perceive.

This is because the entire process is subjective and the Personnel Director can only give a value on that favour from their perspective i.e. how large the stamp would be or the value of the stamp if they had given that favour/ additional work. In addition the Personnel Director is also likely to have a Company stamp book on the number of stamps you owe them! I.e. Sick days, additional holidays, bonuses, etc.

This of course would be taken into account and may even be exchanged stamp for stamp when a question of promotion, pay rises or any other benefit arises. Ultimately, this can be even more frustrating since you are highly unlikely to agree with the size, intensity and value of the stamps "they" feel you owe.

As always, it is not the intent of this book to blame society or even create sociological changes, but to <u>help the individual</u> recognise where frustration and disharmony may occur, so that they may take responsibility for and enhance their life. Ultimately this <u>will benefit society</u> and changes will occur naturally, since if the majority of individual members of society are happy and well balanced then that particular society will gravitate towards happiness and balance.

Although we have focused on negative stamps, it should be noted that it is possible to give and receive positive stamps.

[This process is often used commercially where staff are encouraged to give positive stamps to their customers; when a customer perceives that they are receiving **genuine** positive stamps they will remain loyal to that company **even if the product is second rate!**]

Stamp Collecting directly supports Scripts.

In a first degree Script we may exchange a couple of stamps, perhaps even a page of stamps. As with all references to first degree whether Game Playing, Scripts, Stamp Collecting etc. these actions are usually just a nuisance. This type of stamp exchange is usually connected to minor arguments, disagreements, irritability, perhaps even PMT.

In a second degree process, we may exchange a couple of pages or a whole section of stamps.

Whereas in a third degree process we may close the book, or even the entire collection.

For example: -

First degree: you collect two/ three negative stamps in a minor argument with your partner, on the way to work you collect two more stuck in traffic. At work you exchange/ trade-in your four/ five stamps either one at a time (perhaps being snidey to colleagues), or all at once, by telling off or picking on someone, by minor sabotage where you mess up a letter, or go to lunch early having an extended lunch hour etc.

Second degree: you have been saving up stamps perhaps four or five per day at work for months. A new post is available in another department. You apply for the position only to be told that you need to put a bit more effort in before you might be considered when the next position becomes available. You find yourself in a bad mood and whilst driving home erratically you nudge another car causing damage to your own car and delaying you on your journey home.

It is as if at this point you have picked up another entire page of stamps and someone now owes you. Perhaps you stop at a bar to calm down or as soon as you get home have a good stiff drink to settle your nerves.

Your partner and children have seen this routine before and become very quiet and withdrawn. It is only a matter of time before you verbally lay in to everyone around you, attempting to exchange all of your stamps with your partner and children. Although this will become a bad habit often becoming more aggressive verbally, occasionally even physically; it is unlikely to occur to you, that your partner and children cannot accept "work" stamps. Because of this you are unable to redeem any of your stamp books created at work so you constantly react poorly to unfair situations at work. In addition your work attitude will gradually become unacceptable thereby barring you from any possible chance of promotion.

You, however, are totally unaware of your actions or the driving force behind your actions. This prevents you from enjoying life with a tolerant and happy attitude.

As this is a second degree process then yourself, your partner and your children begin to exist rather than live.   There is a constant atmosphere of worry and fear at home. If this process is prolonged it will eventually deteriorate into a third degree, where either your partner or your Company will eventually meet you in court.

It may even lead to death but not necessarily yours.   Your partner and children are picking up all the wrong messages and one of them may commit suicide. Or perhaps you will storm off in a drunken rage and run some innocent victim over whilst driving under the influence of alcohol. Remember third degree processes generally result in court appearances/ divorce/ prison and/ or death.

*Generally the type of preferred Stamp, the method of redemption of the Stamps, the nature of collection, etc. are dictated by the type of Script the person is running. I.e. Someone running a "Homer Simpson Script may **prefer** to collect "stupid" stamps, but if no stupid stamps were available he could accept "angry" stamps instead. Both meet the needs of that type of Script. Perhaps a Homer Simpson type of Script would need 60% stupid stamps, 20% angry stamps, 10% envy stamps and 10% of miscellaneous stamps.*

Regardless of the degree, a warning is sometimes given that someone is about to "cash in" a stamp book/ collection: -

"Never again", "that's the last time he/ she/ they …!", "that's the last straw!", "nobody uses me that way and gets away with it!", "enough!", etc.

Sometimes a warning is given when a stamp is about to be cashed in or traded: -

"Don't", "enough", "don't be stupid", etc.

Additionally, our behaviour patterns usually give a warning that stamps/ books are about to be traded in: -

Doors may be slammed, things may be kicked, things are thrown around, the "trader" may be muttering to themselves, pets/ children and partners are shouted at.

A level of irritability/ frustration can easily be recognised in a person's behaviour. However, it is unlikely that the person trading in the stamps will realise this. Sometimes we compensate by adopting socially acceptable forms of stamp trading.

This usually involves some form of competitive behaviour such as sport. Even games like chess can be used to relinquish/ exchange stamps.

Again the behaviour patterns are very similar with lots of shouting, excitement, jumping around etc. People shouting, "Yes! Yes! Yes!" or perhaps punching the air or jumping up and down when they have won a game or point; or their team has won a game or a point. This all helps relieve frustration and when we win or our chosen team wins we somehow feel as if this is one in the eye for those invisible buggers that have tried to grind us down.

More enlightened readers already know that life is neither fair or unfair - it just is. But most of us feel at times as if life is unfair, almost as if we personally have a harder time of it than everyone else does. As we are driven by our feelings rather than by rational thought, it is important to have some way of relieving the pressure so that our feelings do not lead us in the wrong direction. All forms of Adapted Pleasure have the ability to do this, whether it is competitiveness or an act of production. Usually being involved in physical competition relieves inappropriate feelings quicker/ more effectively than observing physical competition. The greater the challenge/ achievement, the higher the relief.

Although the previous examples of stamp collecting involved the work place, we often keep separate collections for different areas of our existence. It is not unusual to have social stamps, relationship stamps, work stamps, food stamps, even DIY stamps. All of which can be exchanged or traded in. i.e. practising your DIY skills you have built yet another set of shelving - unfortunately some of the shelves don't quite match or perhaps aren't quite level. As you attempt to attach one shelf with a screw, the screwdriver slips and you cut your hand open for the umpteenth time.

First degree: -

You curse, throw down the offending tool and go and get some attention for your hand.

Second degree: -

You curse at an innocent bystander; perhaps your partner or one of the children or even the family pet making it quite clear that it is their fault. (Unfortunately, they may begin to believe this.) Over the months you may not notice that the entire family including the family pet if it has a choice, make themselves scarce whenever you suggest you could "fix it".

Your partner may even take to deceiving you by arranging for professionals to deal with household faults.

The plumber/ electrician/ carpenter/ mobile mechanic all find themselves with specific instructions to arrive after you leave for work and to complete the task prior to you returning from work.

At some point your partner will be caught, either through the work receipts or perhaps the plumber/ electrician/ etc. being in situ when you arrive home. In second degree this sets a lovely scene for lots of stamps to be demanded immediately. Usually through a series of accusations and/ or an argument (often involving Game Playing).

Third degree: -

In extreme anger you throw the screwdriver away from you perhaps without looking in that direction. The offending weapon strikes your partner, children or family pet leading to injury or even death.

Or perhaps your partner attempts to kindly suggest that since you keep injuring yourself through DIY it might be better to bring in professionals. This causes an extreme reaction/ rage where you may lash out at your partner perhaps forgetting that you have the screwdriver in your hand.
The court appearance is inevitable although it could be for assault, manslaughter, cruelty to animals, or divorce.

Luckily since for many of us DIY is a type of hobby rather than a necessity (often the tools equipment and materials purchased from suitable shops cost more in the long term than using professionals) we usually limit our involvement to first and second degree.
Often as soon as the job becomes too painful or too difficult, and before too many stamps have been collected, we give up.

Usually in the most macho way we can get away with [sorry guys, but is more common for men to do this!]: -

"It needs a reverse thrust universal generator with internal torque control, I don't have that kind of equipment. I mean, I **could** do it if I wanted to, but the generator is too expensive to buy it for a 'one off' job. [In a resigned voice; you know the one, I really, really, wanted to fix this myself but] suppose I'd better call in a plumber/ electrician/ builder/ mechanic/ etc."

Unfortunately, our relationship/ marriage and our children are not hobbies and cannot easily be given up; therefore serious Stamp Collecting in these circumstances is extremely dangerous for our family's health.

Additionally, our work is rarely a hobby and again can rarely be given up; perversely, serious Stamp Collecting in this circumstance is also extremely dangerous for our family's health. Since we often feel that it is difficult to redeem work stamps without threatening future promotion or pay rises, we attempt to exchange or trade them in at home. As this is unlikely we drift into chronic second degree Stamp Collecting/ Game Playing, once again taking things out on our family and friends.

All is not lost!

The archetypal image of "good ol' boys" in southern states (of the USA) all standing around, beers in hand, running down the President, the country, Vietnam, the Gulf war, commies, and anyone else that they would like to have ago at, is actually quite a healthy situation. This is a process in TA nicknamed "pastiming" that both generates positive Strokes and relieves tension.

Even though the conversation is rarely politically correct and often quite extreme, it serves a valuable and important purpose in letting off steam.

Surely it is better for people to verbally lash out at amorphous bodies, to let off steam and get life's unfairness out of their system than to store it all up, until without warning it is all thrown verbally and perhaps even physically at an innocent party.

[Obviously, a balance is required and as long as all the participants consciously or unconsciously recognise that it is just to relieve pent up emotion, things are fine. It is only in the rare and unlikely event that one of the participants takes the conversation seriously and genuinely believes the President should be shot/ all commies should be nuked/ all life's problems have been caused by "Pinko liberalist social workers"/ etc. that this becomes unhealthy and potentially dangerous.

However, this rare complication usually occurs when the participants are already members of extremist groups or organisations.]

Without an understanding of our own behaviour and actions, Stamp Collecting causes unbelievable stress, misery, frustration and unhappiness. Life truly **feels** so unfair. Why me? Its almost as if the Gods have decided to take a personal and unhealthy interest in your life. You were due that promotion, you felt you were promised that promotion and fate/ god/ whatever just floated down and whisked it away. Or the divorcee you were chasing, all that work you put in to pursuing him/ her; then that prat/ tart just wandered into their lives and whisked him/ her away. Or you've just got out of debt after six long years and in the same week the car breaks down, the washing machine dies and your company sacks you. "**Thank you, God! Just what I needed!**". It all seems so personal, so unfair. Nobody else seems to have these trials and tribulations quite like you, in fact *some* people never seem to have problems! If you believe in Karma, you resign yourself to the obvious fact that in a past life you were clearly some kind of "evil baby eating mass murderer" that you now need to atone for, to deserve your present life.

Stamp Collecting is one of the processes that supports Losing Scripts and Game Playing leading to relationship problems and a habit of existing rather than living.

Occasionally in third degree; Stamp Collecting leads to public displays of violence where a person cashing in their entire collection may gun down innocent people in restaurants, schools or out on the streets. Whilst thankfully this is still rare, until a psychology such as TA is taught in school in such a way that it can be used this horrifying behaviour will continue.

In addition individually targeted acts of violence such as road rage will also continue.

Stamps have an emotional value therefore they are <u>felt</u>; no matter how illogical the feeling, we are still *driven* by our **feelings** rather than rational thought.

As was discussed in Parent, Adult and Child our ability to access the conscious Parent and Child and then affect the Parent and Child is directly connected to our Stroke balance and any perceived stress or pressure. The greater the stress or pressure, the less Child and Parent we can access. As the Stroke balance continues to decrease and the stress/ pressure increases we reach a stage where we react purely as the animals we truly are.

Most omnivorous/ carnivorous animals will lash out if hurt.

Our unconscious mind adopts the same behaviour.
There comes a point when our Stamp books are full and there is nowhere to turn, reacting as a cornered animal in pain, we lash out at the source of that pain.
For some people, this is society and is therefore represented by archetypes of society i.e. families in restaurants, children in school, people going about their normal daily business in high streets.
This is one of the reasons why these groups are so easily targeted.

Where this occurs on a smaller/ individual basis, then the person causing your pain is often unconsciously represented by your partner. This is usually untrue, but whether they actually cause you pain or merely fail to relieve your pain by taking your Stamps off you, it is irrelevant. They are still fair game and an easy target. The same rules apply to children and pets being easy targets.
Whilst this is all very depressing, it should be noted that Stamp Collecting has the potential to cause extreme and dramatic acts of random kindness and love.

If Stamp Collecting was taught at school in a way that it could be <u>used</u> then children could be taught to give and therefore collect **positive** stamps.

After a while they would wish to cash in their books.

This may sound like naiveté but imagine the scene: someone carrying ten years of excessive love/ kindness/ happiness/ caring/ joy type stamps wishes to off-load these on to the general public.

With genuine care/ fondness people may be *driven* to care for strangers, to share with neighbours, to genuinely help those in need with no requirement for any form of reward, other than the sheer pleasure of carrying out that care and support for others. Remember we are *driven* by our **feelings** [and our **unconscious** mind], not rational thought.

If we perceive that life is unfair and it becomes a never-ending source of pain, then the build up of these feelings will always lead ultimately to pain.
However, if we perceive that given the chance life is fair and it becomes a never ending source of pleasure, love, kindness etc. then the build up of these feelings will always lead ultimately to the release and sharing of more pleasure, love, kindness etc.

We will be *driven* to be kind. We will be *driven* to happiness. We will be *driven* to love.

Our own unconscious minds will take us step by step to these new destinations.

Perhaps to begin with we may only share this extra love, kindness; etc. with our partners and children but eventually it will spread to everyone that we come into contact with.

Please read this: -

Strangely, one of the best places to start would be the USA, where people through the Constitution have the genuine right and freedom to follow these ideas.

Sadly, in countries like the United Kingdom the residents are *owned* in that they are truly subjects and therefore **subjected** to whatever rule, regulation or whim percolates down from the Monarchy (and those powers representing the Monarchy). Changes in education/ health/ etc. are slower, often more difficult, but not impossible.

It is therefore hoped that sufficient small pockets of resistance (i.e. groups of enlightened people) throughout the UK may build up enough support to put the ideas of W3M™ into local educational programmes, before the authorities can stop them.

It may seem strange that the powers that be, may want to stop people being happy, but at present the UK educational process is more specifically geared to producing "good workers" than it is to produce happy, well-balanced individuals.

In addition the original TA has been promoted to the educational system (there were TA books specifically for the education system, for teachers and for children, have you seen one? I doubt it.) for almost forty years.

As I mentioned on the opening page it was *stolen*, re-written and kept for academics. [Because it works there is big money in TA.]

Well you're three quarters of your journey through this book; make your own mind up, is really "too complicated"?

Do you need "years of training" before you could use some of this?

Does it really have "no practical value"? (I've written this as a "What is" book rather than a "How to" book, but even without the actual step by step instructions of how to change things, the average reader ought to have seen **something** useful? And even if you didn't, surely you can see how some things could be useful?)
And why should you be qualified before you use TA? Unless it is for academia to make yet more money out of you.

After all you bought this book, why shouldn't you use the information in it? If it was a cookery / DIY/ art/ craft/ etc. book no one would expect you to have a university degree before you could use it.

You could have been taught TA freely through school at any time in the past thirty to forty years. There is a book TA for Tots by Alvyn M. Freed Phd, Jalmar Press 1976 [sadly now out of print] so children could even learn TA at nursery school.

[Alvyn M Freed Phd produced a dozen perfectly good books; records, cassettes and multimedia on TA all aimed at Tots, Kids and Teenagers.]

Think of how different your life could have been?

What your childhood might have been like? In particular if you are young enough that **your** parents may have been taught TA, what your childhood might have been like then?

Your marriage might have been?

How enjoyable, secure, satisfying your work could have been?

Think of how different Society would be?

Do you **really** want **your** children to grow up not knowing these things? Making the same mistakes? Often existing instead of being happy?

Make yourself a promise [and keep it!]. Promise yourself, for you, for your kids, whatever, that you will learn and use the information in this book to make your life [and in turn your loved ones, lives] better.
There is no need to hurt; there is no need to suffer.
Losers hurt! Losers suffer! Winners get out there and kick butt!

Losers "win or lose", "succeed of fail". Winners "win or learn", "succeed or learn".

Learn: Succeed: Win.

P.P.P.'s

- All Stamps have a subjective value.

- Stamps usually have an emotive charge connected to them. I.e. Anger.

- People collect Stamps habitually. A preference for certain types of Stamp and a preference for certain sources of Stamp. I.e. Anger Stamps collected at work. Or fear Stamps collected at home.

- There are three degrees of Stamp Collecting/ Trading.

- Small problems occur with first degree Stamp Collecting/ Trading. Big problems occur with third degree Stamp Collecting/ Trading.

- Redeeming/ Trading one or two stamps is usually first degree. A full page or entire section is usually second degree. Whilst redeeming entire albums is usually third degree.

- Stamps are usually collected when we have put ourselves out in some way for others, or when something occurs that we could have done without. I.e. we do an extra ten hours per week on a project at work, outside of our normal hours. The company* now owes us a Stamp that is worth ten hours of extra work/ any new skill we had to learn/ any extra hassle involved/ the argument we had with our partner because of the extra hours/ the special edition of our favourite TV programme that we missed through working late [although we got some of that back, having a go at our partner because they didn't record it!]/ etc.

- Even if companies realised that their staff collect Stamps, we still may not get the Trade in value that we expect.

- Where Stamp Collecting is understood and applied, positive Stamps can be collected instead of negative Stamps.

---

* We often "Stamp" the company rather than the person who asked us, since we perceive that this work was carried out for the company's benefit.

133

- The Script/ s we run normally dictate the type of Stamps that we collect.

- Recognisable warnings are usually given when someone is about to "cash in"/ trade Stamps. These can be verbal, behavioural, emotional, and often all three.

- Competitive sports/ hobbies can allow safe Stamp reduction/ exchange.

- Past-timing is a particularly healthy/ safe way to let go of Stamps.

- In extreme cases third degree Stamp Collecting can result in public displays of violence; where families in restaurants, children at school, innocent bystanders will be gunned down.

- In second degree Stamp Collecting our own loved ones are usually the targets for verbal/ physical/ mental abuse.

- Stamps have an emotional value, since we are *driven* through how we **feel**, most acts connected to Stamp Collecting are irrational.

Aspects of TA as shown through W3M^{TM} ^{are} easily learnt and have a practical application. [Often just by learning TA we feel better.]:-

1. Collect positive Stamps instead of negative.

2. Identify which mind you are weakest [or have a problem in] and strengthen it.

3. Identify Games others draw you into and deal with them accordingly.

4. Increase your positive Stroke balance and/ or reduce your negative Stroke balance.

5. If your partner has crossed *the* Point of Commitment, recognise that their actions are thoughtless rather than vindictive and deal with it accordingly.

6. If you have a not OK Child mind help it to grow/ develop and remember that nine out of ten people that you know, also have a not OK Child to some degree. Etc.

FRAMES OF REFERENCE

Frames of Reference (<u>complex</u>) are the conscious mind's ability to evidence to the unconscious mind what is real or unreal.

The unconscious mind (which uses <u>basic</u> Frames of Reference) is unable to recognise reality without the conscious minds assistance.

In fact, most thoughts, feelings and images as perceived through the unconscious mind, perhaps even originated by the unconscious mind are accepted as real.

We use Frames of Reference to allow us to confirm or deny that which is around us. In effect we use these ideas to confirm that which is real for us.

This is an important aspect of survival; if we cannot confirm or deny our reality and therefore perceive it as a threat, then our survival mechanism will respond accordingly even though no true physical threat exists.

Please read this: -

Using a nightmare as an example: when we go to sleep we do not normally expect to create or to be subjected to a nightmare.

Whilst we are asleep our conscious awareness is unavailable and we are subject to our "guardians of sleep" [Freud 1856-1939]. These "guardians" create scenes that are so vivid and real in their nature that occasionally we are awakened to deal directly with them.

Even if such images are mythical to the **Adult mind** perhaps Dragons, Goblins and Fairies; we accept them as real in our sleep/ unconsciousness mind.

Using basic Frames of Reference (senses) such as touch, taste, sight, smell, and fake Frames of Reference (emotions) such as fear our unconscious mind makes the Dragon real.

We can *feel* the hot breath of the Dragon, we *smell* the rotting flesh in it's teeth, *feel* the razor sharpness of it's claw touching our shin, *hear* its heavy breathing. It's slaver drips onto our face- we *feel* the heat - the wet - the burning pain from the acid dripping from its mouth, etc.

Movement is fast and furious in nightmare situations we are often overwhelmed by the incoming evidence. Everything is real, solid. There is rarely a second that we recognise that it is a nightmare. In some particularly invidious nightmares we become "lucid", aware that it is only a nightmare, we wake up with relief only to find that we didn't wake at all and we are still in the nightmare! The sheer intensity of fear, it is totally **real** to the unconscious mind.

In that short period between being involved in the nightmare and being wide-awake, the nightmare is **real**.

I.e. we respond as if it is a genuine threat to our survival:-

Raised heartbeat, shallow and rapid breathing, heightened sense of awareness, terrified, screaming, got to get away, escape, becoming so terrified that fighting back doesn't occur to us, etc.

It is only **after** we have applied the **complex** Frames of Reference in our **Adult mind** that we can begin to calm down.

In fact, it is only our complex Frames of Reference that allow us to discount the nightmare and begin to calm down. [It was basic Frames of Reference that allowed the unconscious mind to create the nightmare in the first place. **That** is why it was so real!]

In this example, our complex Frames of Reference would have included:-

Familiar surroundings, time, plus the recognition that aspects of the nightmare are incongruous and/ or out of synch with our normal environment.

*Without these essential skills we would **continue to respond to a nightmare as if it were real.***

Without complex Frames of Reference, how would we know what is real and what isn't? People with limited/ damaged complex Frames of Reference really will see Dragons, Goblins and Fairies.!

[This may be used as a simple explanation of certain types of mental illness in that the sufferer has incomplete or different Frames of Reference from the majority of the population. They continue to react to a reality that is individual/unique to themselves. Although we all do this to some degree; we tend to use Frames of Reference that are common to the "group" (i.e. taught/observed in childhood) and we therefore appear sane.]

"Without complex Frames of Reference, how would we know what is real and what isn't?" [Self-portrait of Frank and ~~fiends~~ friends. Using complex Frames of Reference I can tell the picture isn't real:- Frank doesn't have that much hair! ☹ Sorry Frank, I couldn't resist that one.]

We constantly meddle with our Frames of Reference whether it is through direct access such as hypnosis/ counselling or indirectly through the media i.e. television and films.

The obvious implication that this will affect our sanity and in certain cases can quite literally unhinge us, doesn't seem to prevent people from charging off quite happily to watch violence and fearful subjects at the cinema.

Whilst the media that we allow ourselves to be affected by is self inflicted and therefore perhaps acceptable, the use of mind altering drugs often prescribed by GPs is not. It also stands to reason that the use of "street drugs" is also unacceptable. Many of these types of drugs cause permanent changes to our ability to establish a frame of reference.

It should also be noted that psychiatrists, certain types of psychologist, counsellors, hypnotherapists, etc. all constantly meddle directly with their clients' Frames of Reference.

Whilst most have good intentions that such meddling will provide a positive result and their client will improve accordingly, there is still no evidence that this is true.

In fact, many practitioners realise that their therapy often causes a knock-on or permanent perhaps even unwanted effect to their clients' Frames of Reference. However, most justify their actions by claiming that the change affects the person in the here and now and that any future problems could be worked upon at a later date.

Obviously this claim does not negate any social problems where their client's family, friends, work colleagues could all be affected through their therapy. Yet these people are hardly likely to approach these practitioners for treatment to repair any damage caused through the original client.

Think about it for a moment.

How would we react if our fears, anxieties and symptoms etc. were removed from all areas of our lives?

Many people receiving character reinforcement for anxiety connected to a specific action or scenario, appear to be more able to assert themselves, are happier, become optimistic, become less introverted, etc. within days of their first session; even though the original treatment was specifically aimed at one symptom and in fact that particular symptom may not have improved at this point.

What is worse, these changes are often noticed by the people around the client, rather than the client themselves. This suggests that the client has changed in some recognisable way even though they are unaware of it.

Cause and effect cannot easily be recognised, as the person involved may have demonstrated these abilities prior to the original symptoms (but been unaware of this) OR may have developed them as a direct result of a change in their Frames of Reference. This suggests that our Frames of Reference are linked and it may be difficult is even impossible to affect one without it having some kind of affect on the others.

Sometimes our Frames of Reference are so powerful they create a different form of reality to everyone else.

As a general rule of thumb psychotics have different and often more entrenched Frames of Reference than neurotics.

If we help someone affected through neurosis to change their Frames of Reference, then we are often gradually pushing them towards psychosis.

Since Frames of Reference, perceived from this understanding, allow us to identify or discount reality, there are a limited number of Frames of Reference that can be altered before we are no longer "us".

After all, one's sense of self is created through one's individual and selective Frames of Reference!

If you are worried/ insecure/ feel you can't cope and either through drugs or a counsellor, you change your Frames of Reference and you now feel more in control, assertive and less anxious, then surely that can't be a bad thing? Yet your entire attitude and behaviour will change. The way you deal with your family will change and at the end of the day how much is enough? After all, few people suffering from psychosis demonstrate anxiety or are unable to assert themselves!

139

The simple truth is no one really knows whether we should or shouldn't dabble with our Frames of Reference.

However, we need to accept that there is a constant process of erosion carried out against our Frames of Reference both from legal and illegal sources, whether it be drugs or television, the eventual effects are similar.

Whilst basic Frames of Reference are created in our Child and Parent minds, the ability to affect them consciously is part of the role of the Adult mind.

In addition, more complicated Frames of Reference are developed in the Adult.

This is supported by the nightmare example where basic [Child and Parent mind] Frames of Reference were used to create the nightmare in the first place. As the nightmare began to take on a life of its own, we are awakened so that the Adult mind may override the Child or Parent response. A new set of Frames of Reference is then applied. We need sufficient time using our conscious mind to identify that we are in familiar and hopefully different surroundings from those offered in the nightmare. We need sufficient **conscious** ability to recognise that the main subjects in the nightmare are incongruous i.e. if the nightmare involves tigers or dragons and we do not normally have tigers or dragons living in our bedroom then our conscious Adult can start to discount the evidence we see before our eyes.

Basic Frames of Reference are connected to our five senses, and in our early life this is exactly how they are established.

If as a toddler you are wandering around a room and bang your head on a table, then this is a very efficient and quick way of establishing a Frame of Reference as to whether the table exists or not.

Part of our visual perception is also used to establish Frames of Reference.

In the early days, a baby may reach out to hold an object that may be several feet away from him, or reach beyond an object that is only inches away from their eyes. As the baby creates their Frames of Reference in regard to their spatial awareness, then they will no longer reach beyond an object or mistakenly believe they can grasp an object beyond their reach since part of their mind can now evidence the position of the things around them.

P.P.P.'s

- Basic Frames of Reference (FoR's) are created in the unconscious Child and Parent in early childhood.

- **Basic** FoR's use the five senses to identify reality.

- Basic FoR's are regularly scaled down in intensity so that the conscious mind is not overwhelmed.

- **False** FoR's use emotions to identify reality.

- **Fake** FoR's use a platform such as "Science" to construct a new reality.

- Without FoR's the unconscious mind will perceive **all** internal images as reality.

- **Complex** FoR's are created in the Adult.

- Complex FoR's are used by the *conscious* mind to identify reality.

- The conscious mind creates an individual reality using basic and complex FoR's. Therefore reality is a series of myths that overlap. [Too deep? Because every person's conscious mind has different FoR's both in intensity and nature, each person *constructs* their own individual perception of reality, from both incoming data and their unconscious filter program.]

- FoR's are the secret keys to the soul. I.e. What each of us is "touched" by, or what affects us most is personal and individual.

- In fact some religions [such as Buddhism] encourage ignoring/ closing down certain FoR's so that a glimpse of the *true* reality is gained.   I.e. Enlightenment is a fragmentary condition where *truth* just *is;* it is quite literally *"blindingly clear"*. Since without considerable mental discipline our FoRs regain control rapidly, blinding us once again.
- Where there are shared/ common FoR's these are part of the human condition.

141

POINTS OF COMMITMENT

Even a modest glance at human behaviour would demonstrate an unconscious Point of Commitment. With everyone, adult or child there comes a point in their behaviour where they are now totally committed to a course of action or a task in hand. Many of these things are seen in the smaller scale of things through the unconscious Parent. As mentioned in a previous chapter the Parent mind is responsible for *doing things.* There comes a point where we are aware that an every day task needs to be carried out. At this point the unconscious Parent mind reaches a "Point of Commitment" and our entire energy and efforts are devoted often without conscious thought to the completion of said task. Within Transactional Analysis there is a second type of Point of Commitment, this being on a much larger scale.

If the Point of Commitment is in a relationship, then from the point of commitment onwards, the partner that has reached this Point of Commitment is now totally committed to the relationship.

Although one would expect this to be the point of marriage or perhaps when a couple move in together, this is rarely the case. It should also be noted that everyone reaches their Points of Commitment at a different stage to the other people involved in their lives.

A Point of Commitment may be reached in any sphere of our existence whether this is with our job, with our children, with our partner, our friends, a hobby, or any other part of our lives.

To begin with you may find this a peculiar idea to come to terms with?

Surely we will be committed to our relationship if we get married?

Are we not committed to our children merely by the biological process of producing them?

Why would we have a hobby if we were not committed to it?

Or friends for that matter, if we are not committed to them?

These simple myths could not be further from the truth!

Just looking a little deeper reveals that many people are not committed to the things they are associated with. If you think carefully it becomes obvious, after all if someone was committed to their relationship why would they be unfaithful?

Yet every day, hundreds of thousands of people throughout the world betray their partners!

If people were truly committed to their children, why would they leave them with others whilst they pursue their careers?

Just stop for a moment and look at your behaviour, do you **claim** to love someone yet you constantly put *your* needs first?

Do you claim you want promotion at work yet regularly arrive *late/ leave early/ work half-heartedly?*

Do you say you want to change in some way yet never *take the action* that would allow that change?

Perhaps you also haven't reached the right Point of Commitment?

*Throughout this chapter and in fact throughout any aspect of TA, it should be recognised that the entire process of "Points of Commitment" is usually **unconscious**. However, by becoming aware that such a process exists allows us to lessen the severity of this change and to compensate accordingly. It should also be noted that without conscious awareness of going through a "Point of Commitment" the individual involved has **no** conscious understanding or awareness that they have changed.*

It may be useful at this moment to recognise that we not only go through a "Point of Commitment" at some stage in any new venture but we can also close down a previously established "Point of Commitment" at a certain stage in any venture.

This is fairly easy to recognise in relationships where a couple may fall in love, commit to marriage, fall out of love and commit to divorce.

It can also easily be seen in our choice of careers where we may throw ourselves wholeheartedly into the process of ambition/ advancement and are clearly committed at that moment to our chosen profession. At some point for whatever reason, our commitment is lost/ fails and we no longer pursue advancement. In fact, we may actually choose an entirely different profession.

In popular psychology, people talk about the "seven-year itch" in marriage; "mid-life crisis" where previously apparently sane people suddenly wish for a new/ younger partner or career or even both.

The "seven-year itch" may occur because the partner has either not reached the Point of Commitment in their relationship, or has closed down a Point of Commitment that they had previously established.

Whereas a "mid-life crisis" is usually (but not always) where a previous Point of Commitment has failed; or worse still, purely through the recognition of the passage of time it has just closed down.

At any stage in our lives we always have a certain balance between our Parent, Adult and Child minds. We may for example, have adopted 60% Parent, 20% Adult and 20% Child for our every day activities. Or we may have 20% Parent, 20% Adult and 60% Child* in our relationship with our partner.

It is important to consider these division/ percentages as averages at that stage in our lives/ relationships, since on any given day the balances will change.

*Where one partner has a dominant Parent [perhaps 60%] and the other partner has a matching dominant Child [60%] they are considered to be in *symbiosis*. As such it is the relationship that has a balance of minds not the individual. Provided both partners are comfortable with their share of Parent/ Child then the relationship can plod along quite comfortably for many years. However if the point of commitment is reached by the dominant Child partner after this stage, then considerable problems can occur. Similarly where a partner is forced into the dominant Child role, because the other partner has reached a point of commitment, then serious resentment and *stamp collecting* will occur.

Using a relationship as an example, as a general rule of thumb, most people fall in love through a high percentage of positive Child activity therefore both partners may have 10% Parent, 20% Adult and <u>70% Child</u> whilst they are *in love*.

Later, as the relationship enters a more secure phase, partners although still loving each other but not being in that heady period of being *in love* may adopt 15% Parent, 35% Adult and 50% Child. However, at the moment that one of the partners reaches their point of commitment, the balance may become (literally overnight) 70% Parent, 20% Adult and 10% Child.

The partner in this example has no conscious recognition that they have changed but their other half now feels that they are married to/ living with a completely different person.

Whereas before they were fun loving, exciting to be with, sexually active/ adventurous; their partner is now serious, perhaps to the point of appearing "middle-aged" overnight. Physical contact is reduced, replaced by long periods of silence and coldness.

Although this is perhaps more reasonably described as thoughtlessness to the partner on the receiving end of 70% Parent, it feels like their partner is uncaring perhaps even to the point of vindictiveness. Ironically, it is the initial partner's unconscious commitment to the relationship that may now push the other partner away.

Practical: -

Try and create the following images in your mind:

You are 19 and have met the person of your dreams. They are exciting, fun loving and [perhaps far more importantly] accept you for just being you. All you can think of over the next few weeks is this person. You are waiting for them to phone, waiting to meet, and in between meetings practically put your life on hold. Gradually, you see more and more of each other and become "an item". Although you are still *in love* you may consider the future, what you would both like to do, where you may end up, what wonderful adventures you could have.

During this period, we often head into a more long-term relationship, perhaps moving in together or getting married.

Things are all so very exciting and fun. Money is there to be spent either on each other or in a pursuit of fun. Basically, life is good and you feel good. You also feel free, free to discuss intimate desires, personal hopes, dreams, wishes, perhaps even totally free to offer your opinion on anyone or anything.

This is a rare, precious and endangered stage in your life.

As a child you would rarely have been allowed to give your **genuine** opinion on family members, you certainly wouldn't have felt comfortable sharing intimate desires, personal hopes and dreams with your siblings or your parents. True, you often discussed "safe" subjects with your family but many things are held back.

Suddenly, you are sharing your life with this marvellous and loving person that you can share *any thought* no matter how intimate *without fear or judgement*.

Just think of how wonderfully, "touchy-feely" this stage of the relationship is? You can barely keep your hands off each other, you are overwhelmed by a surplus of strokes and you feel wonderful. In fact you may feel wonderful just *thinking* about this person.

Then one day, they wake up, get up and go about their early morning routine without the lengthy but very pleasant touchy-feely type process we often have when we are first in love. You may think nothing of it, but as the days go by and you realise that they no longer bother to wake you up with a cuddle and nuzzling your face and neck, you begin to worry.

In fact, not only has the intimate morning wake-up vanished, but so has most of the physical process. The constant touches no matter what your activities have now gone, the regular glances and other evidence of love has vanished into thin air.

Your partner ridicules your opinions or "fixes" things you may have been upset or bothered by or dismisses the things you say as childish or naïve.

Permissible conversation subjects now include household finances and expenditure, insurance, budgets, work, perhaps even politics and sport.

Things that were never mentioned or even considered in those first heady days/ weeks/ months.

Worse still your partner now just does things, without even involving you in the process.

Mornings have become cold, silent affairs with monosyllable answers if any.

You begin to question yourself or your partner "Why are they so different?" "Is it something I've have done?" "Do they have eyes for someone else?" "Why do I feel so unloved?"

As this condition drags on you may begin to question whether it is worth remaining in the relationship. Clearly your partner no longer loves you and hasn't loved you for a long time.

Although you are using your imagination, if this really happens to you, *you would be* **stunned** *to discover that your partner* **believes** *they still love you, and has* <u>no idea</u> *of how you feel, nor do they have* <u>any idea</u> *that the relationship has changed.*

This is an example of a percentage change in your Parent, Adult, and Child minds through the Point of Commitment.

The morning your partner woke up, got up, and just got on with things was the first morning after the unconscious Point of Commitment had been made. This wonderful exciting person that you fell in love with; you fell in love with **because** of such a high percentage of **Child** + Adult activity, perhaps 70% Child, 20-25% Adult and the remainder Parent.

Now you find yourself living with some cold-blooded reptile with 70% Parent, 20-25% Adult and the remainder Child.

Your partner now has completely different attitudes, ideas and interests.

They have become judgmental and opinionated.

They are often convinced at this stage that their opinions are right and are the best for both them and you. Decisions may be made at this point without your involvement. Like a child you are informed of each new situation **after** it has been actioned.

You **know** that this is not the person you fell in love with and in a strange way, you are right.

The fact that you could help them return to that fun-loving person probably wouldn't occur to you. [See the "how to book" when it's written. Ed.]

All you know is that you have to get away from them or change the situation.

They **know** that they are the same person because they have always had their Parent mind. Therefore they have always held these opinions and attitudes. They believe implicitly that you knew this when you committed yourself to them. And in a strange way *they* are wrong. What they are unaware of is that they rarely had an opportunity to display such an intense Parental attitude and that such thoughts/ opinions were always in the back of the Parent mind. Sadly, they may see their partner as slightly "dippy", childish or not quite "all there". Far more dangerously they may even come to believe that their partner is incapable or even mentally ill. After all, with that degree of Parentalness, if their partner cannot see why their opinion is right, then they **must be** *ill [mentally]*.

This sad knowledge has been known for many years, yet how often at school/ college, are we taught how to prevent it? Or avoid this particular Point of Commitment, perhaps even to reverse the Point of Commitment?

Why shouldn't we be happily in love throughout our entire relationship?

Why is it frowned upon in our society to remain blissfully happy with our chosen partner?

Many professions tend towards Parentalness: -

Police, Lawyers, Doctors, Nurses, Teachers, etc.

Psychiatry is one of the more extreme Parental professions.

Until very recently, it has not been too difficult to convince a psychiatrist that your partner is ill/ unable to cope merely because they didn't share yours (and your psychiatrist's!) Parental attitudes and opinions.

After all one of the great joys of the Parent mind is an unshakeable belief that **you** are OK and it is everyone else that has got a problem.

Since many Parental concepts (duty, loyalty, responsibility etc.) are common, then Parental professions tend to share the same concepts.

The Parent mind conveniently forgets how exciting and sweet a partner was when they were going to be an artist, a musician, or a poet. It [the Parent mind] now has little tolerance for such childish fantasies. After all isn't it about time their partner got a "proper" job and contributed to the household income.

Tens of thousands, perhaps even hundreds of thousands of wonderfully creative potential musicians, writers, poets and authors have succumbed to the Parental onslaught of both their partners and society.

The potential pleasures, joy and genuine artistic benefits for society that have been lost through Parental behaviour are heart breaking. We are so busy chasing responsibilities and what we *should do,* that we forget or lose pleasures in life and what we **could** do.

Whether it could be argued that this results from the individual's Point of Commitment in a relationship, or perhaps a Point of Commitment to society, is irrelevant. The fact remains that through the Point of Commitment, **things change** whether it be a relationship or society as a whole.

Worrying about which comes first should be the realm of academia.

In real life, we have to live with our partner's changes and the changing attitudes within society. It is essential that an understanding of the Point of Commitment, and the effect that it has on each of us, be accepted by both parties!

As argued earlier by understanding that a Point of Commitment is on the horizon, you could avert it or compensate for it.

Provided we are not harming others does it **really** matter if we remain happily *in love*?

Is it **really** such a big deal if we were to enjoy our entire lives being in love and happy?

Even if this does mean we may make the occasional poor financial decision?

Or that we may appear a little "dippy" and fun loving?

Or that we may not be as dedicated to Parental issues as society is at the moment?

After all it is an argument in W3M^{TM} that many of society's ills are pre-programmed through observations of our parents or other significant adults, when we are children. Surely if our parents are truly in love and happy and therefore we both feel and observe that we are to be in love and happy, then the world would become a better place.

This does not mean that all of society's ills would be fixed overnight but the ones connected to our present method of upbringing would be affected.

Most of societies problems connected to relationships and their subsequent breakdowns would also be resolved.

Whilst the point of commitment has the potential to bring security, it is more often the trigger for unhappiness.

The Child mind is very much like two sides of a coin. Whilst the coin is on its edge, it could fall either way.

One face represents pain and the avoidance thereof whilst the other represents pleasure and the pursuit thereof.

When we fall in love, the pleasure side is usually uppermost. However, when our partner reaches their point of commitment, they gradually and unceasingly turn the coin over. Our days become filled with fears, anxiety and depression as the Child is reminded of its original misperception that it is bad and/ or unloved.

After all, our partner no longer touches us, cares for us, and loves us. Isn't this **exactly** how we felt when our first brother or sister arrived and/or we first misperceived that we were **unloved**?

History repeats itself. The lack of physical touch, the periods of coldness, the way our parents just get on with things, almost as if we are now just a nuisance or in the way.

This is the evidence we used as children to prove we were unloved, it is the same evidence we will use as adults to prove we are unloved.

The lack of physical touch, the periods of coldness, the way our partner just gets on with things almost as if we are now just a nuisance or in the way. Sadly familiar. And just like our parents there is <u>always a reason</u>.

Our partners abound with pseudo-legitimate comments; there is **always some excuse.**

As pointed out at the beginning of this chapter a Point of Commitment is reached in any sphere or our existence whether this is with our job, with our children, with our partner, our friends, a hobby or any other part of our lives. We therefore repeat the entire process with and for children. The coldness is there, the lack of physical touch, the lack of time, and the pseudo-legitimate excuses. There is always a reason and in our Parent mind, we believe it implicitly. If our children suffer, if our partner suffers, if our friends suffer, then it is hardly *our fault*? It could only be the way life is and who are we to question the rules of society no matter how cruel they may feel to the people who suffer from them. *[Isn't this the same kind of excuse used by war criminals?]*

The initial emphasis in this chapter was on what the Point of Commitment is. This was expanded into how it affects us. The remainder of this chapter is devoted to how some Point of Commitments occur.

An archetypal image of a 1950's style relationship is used for this example. * [Prior to wide scale use of the contraceptive pill and the social changes this brought about. The Points of Commitment were easily identified during this era, which is why this particular example is used.]

*This section is **not** politically correct by present standards, however it is a fact of history that women had different rights and conditions to men.

WARNING! **If you cannot cope with non-politically correct issues please go to the next chapter!**

For many women in the 1950s and 1960s the Point of Commitment in a relationship would often come at either engagement/ marriage/ or the first sexual encounter.

In a symbolic way and a literal way the female partner in the relationship would quite literally have given herself up at the Point of Commitment.

These Points of Commitment were universal throughout Western Society at this time and her peer group would scorn any woman who failed to evidence passing through the Point of Commitment, when all three of these occasions had passed.

Unfortunately, these opportunities to pass through the Point of Commitment were so rigidly and Parentally observed that failure to complete the ritual could have dire effects.

In the UK today there are still women under psychiatric care when their only "offence" was to fail to know/ marry the father of their child.

Sadly, after receiving 40 or 50 years of psychiatric care, many of these unlucky women are now institutionalised and unlikely to rejoin the rest of society.

Promiscuity was literally perceived as evidence of psychiatric disorder.

Yet many of these women were <u>assumed</u> to be promiscuous, merely by becoming pregnant!

Unless things have changed? I understood that one partner, one sexual experience [without protection] can lead to pregnancy.

Yet becoming pregnant, was accepted by psychiatrists as evidence of promiscuity. Talk about a Parental profession, no trial, no judge, no jury, and no appeal, put away for <u>life</u> for becoming pregnant.

The unconscious choice was simple. **Regardless** of whether the first sexual experience occurred before or after marriage, it was often regarded as the <u>last</u> opportunity to pass through the Point of Commitment.

Men had slightly more choice in that the same three rights of passage could offer an opportunity for the Point of Commitment.

However, two strange additional rights were accorded these being the arrival of the first child, or even the first mortgage. [It's a long story; perhaps I'll explain why it happened in future book. Ed.]

The legacy of this has fuelled the more extreme side of feminism in that some men had not committed themselves (unconsciously) to their partner even though they were married. In their <u>unconscious</u> mind they were still free to explore/ play the field, which unfortunately some men did.

Some of these men would have stopped this behaviour the moment that the first child arrived, or they found themselves committed to a mortgage.

Some men would have left their partners for their mistresses before this point had been reached.

It is quite sad that through the behaviour of a small minority of men that the extremists in feminism have accused all men. There now appears to be a great rush among some women to mimic the supposed/ claimed poor behaviour of men.

If this behaviour was so unacceptable and outrageous, why are some women so keen to become ambitious, aggressive, uncaring, judgmental, patronising, promiscuous, and many of the other things men were accused of?

This exposes the myths that are perpetuated by most extreme groups, and are used to fuel political correctness.

Almost every sociological group has suffered at some point in history: -

"After all, we men suffered terribly, from years of maternal hierarchy from Stone Age tribes through to Celtic society. For many thousands of years, we were kept under the thumb, suffered abuse, beaten, starved both of food and love/ affection, men were prevented from creative and artistic endeavours, men were not allowed positions of power and kept at all times subordinate to women!

This was a very evil, violent and cruel period. The dreadful atrocities afflicted upon young boys and men, by women; are too foul and shocking to be reported in detail in this book!

When the Romans showed that great women leaders could be overthrown and through their occupation of most of Europe eventually brought the hope for men, that God was really a man and not as they had been taught for many thousands of years that God was a woman. Then men threw themselves wholeheartedly into the saving, but paternal religion of Christianity.

Finally, men were able to free themselves from the millennia of lies, cruelty and abuse perpetuated by women.

I now ask all men reading this book, to take their rightful place in society.

And those women that represent the unhappiness and suffering that for so many thousands of years was inflicted upon men, to now take a back seat and let us caring, supporting men run society.

Never again can we allow such evil and fickle creatures that call themselves women, to hold a position in society! In fact we men should be granted compensation for all that dreadful abuse!"

This parody is sad and ridiculous!

The preceding paragraphs are quite truthful, many tribes were Maternal with warrior leaders such as Boudicca aka Boudecia being the norm. In some Mediterranean cultures men were ritually slaughtered, by and/ or on the orders of the female leaders.

But I can hardly imagine millions of men rallying round this banner; so that they could put women in their place, for the cruelty, oppression and lies that men suffered from thousands of years ago.

The simple truth is that by the very nature of our past and the fact that we are mammals first and humans second, that almost everyone has a claim from some point in history that they were put upon by someone else.

Most extremists claim points in history as their defence.

Perhaps in a call for world peace, we should exterminate all Germans since Germany is credited for starting two world wars?

Or we should place a trade embargo on the USA as the only country to use nuclear weapons in war?

Or we should demand restitution from Italy because Rome conquered most of the (then) known world?

Ridiculous isn't it!

But this form of extreme behaviour is worth £/$ billions!

Political Correctness legislated through and from extreme viewpoints brings in and costs £/$ billions.

In the UK some local governments are so keen to be seen as politically correct that they legislate **against** the majority of their constituents.

For many council's their WASP'S (White Anglo-Saxon Protestant) represent 90 - 95% of their constituents; yet these same council's commit 80 – 90% of their reserve budget on minority groups.

These stances have become so extreme that some UK police forces appear to spend as much, if not more on ensuring *political correctness* within the force, than on crime!

Schools and libraries destroy our heritage by banning books that are not politically correct.

On job applications it is no longer acceptable to be British; people in Gt. Britain often have to state their ethnic group, their gender, their sexual bias and whether they are *challenged* in any way.

In our great rush to be Politically Correct we now **patronise** [in its worst sense] minority groups!

What each of these job applications is **really saying** is that if you come from a listed minority group, you are so pathetic you need to state this to have any chance of getting the job! Obviously if anyone from a minority group was actually capable of getting the job, they would not need to declare their position!

Of course Political Correctness only truly works one way; after considerable lobbying by "PC groups" the only single sex colleges [at the time of writing this book] in Oxford are women only! It is **always** acceptable to bar men; it is only unacceptable if **women** are barred. (Perhaps men are less aggressive than women and therefore have less need to create pressure groups?)
Hopefully, this is where common sense can prevail.

One of the aims of this book W3M™ (and an original aim of TA) is that we can modify our behaviour in the <u>present</u>, to gain a higher quality of life for ourselves/ families. Whilst, at the same time, accepting that the very **situation**[*] of early childhood, leaves almost all of us with the need to grieve for our losses.

Whether these be the misperception that we are bad, or the misperception that we are unloved by one or both of our parents, or the scripts that we create in this early period.

Every one of us has the seeds of unhappiness, anxiety, despair and depression sown in those early days of childhood.

We have enough trouble trying to come to terms with and cope with these seeds; without being distracted by who did what to whom, when and where in history.

If we all accept self-responsibility and use a little common sense, then there is little need to legislate in regard to <u>moral</u> conduct (Political Correctness et al).

* It is the **situation** of childhood, the *way* that we develop, the *misunderstanding* by our own parents of our rational capabilities, regardless of the *intent* of our parents, that cause the not OK position in the Child. We can have the most loving attentive parents in the world and we can still adopt the not OK position in the Child.

P.P.P.'s

- Points of Commitment (PoC) are <u>unconscious</u> decisions.

- Although traditionally used to identify changes in relationships, PoC's are connected to all aspects of human behaviour.

- People reach their PoC's at a different point/ time to their partner.

- In cultures with strong moral/ religious attitudes PoC's can be easily identified and are usually universal for that culture.

- Where **moral** issues are legislated for [i.e. Certain forms of Political Correctness.] PoC identification becomes vague.

- **Certain types of PoC support Society** directly; if removed then moral and even legal decay follows quite rapidly.

- Certain types of PoC *damage* relationships; whilst others *support* relationships.

- Where disharmony in a relationship is created through a PoC, then one or both parties lack sufficient *understanding* to cope.

- Most psychotherapy's attempt to recognise and/ or change PoC's.

- Where a person's attitude/ behaviour/ stance/ etc. on any issue changes it usually indicates that a PoC has been reached in regard to that issue.

- If you have strong feelings about this book [positive "Wow! It's really good!"; or negative "What a load of rubbish!"] Then **you** have reached a small PoC!

- PoC's determine the available energy/ motivation available for each specific activity.

- Self-responsibility includes identifying the PoC's we are affected by and taking the appropriate action.

- Just knowing about a PoC can change the effect it has on us.

- PoC's **can** be changed consciously, with a modest amount of common sense and application.

- Certain types of PoC are usually created from the observations of the Parent mind, following what it perceives is the right thing to do.

- Other types of PoC reside in the Child mind.

- Conscious [these are very rare] PoC's can be created in the Adult.

- PoC's **always** result in a change of balance [percentages] in the Parent, Adult and Child minds.

- You *think* you are your Adult mind, but you are actually the sum of your PoC's and your Child. Of course you are *affected* by Strokes, Scripts, Game Playing, Stamp Collecting, etc.
[No example this time you have to do this on your own, think about it! Think about what makes you do things? How do you know what you like/ want/ prefer?]

NEEDS

As was discussed in an earlier chapter, the Child and Parent minds are mammalian whilst the Adult truly allows us to be human. It is therefore important to both recognise and ensure that mammalian needs are tended to enable the Adult mind to function effectively.

There are two different types of needs these being true mammalian needs such as food, warmth, shelter, company etc. and adapted needs connected to pain and pleasure.

As a general rule we tend to these needs automatically by ensuring that we have some kind of accommodation, an adequate food supply and suitable company.

It tends to be threats in connection to this that becomes a problem rather than failing to meet these needs in the first place. I.e. the loss of a job may mean we have to move and may also mean that we have to change the type of food that we are used to. Therefore, the **threat** of redundancy in a Company is enough to begin to cause anxiety within the Child mind usually involving "what if" type fears. It is conscious awareness that allows us to be affected in this negative way since if we could not grasp the idea that our job can be taken away from us then we will be unable to anxiete.

This suggests that anxiety/ worry are meant to fulfil a purpose rather than cause suffering.

If the thought processes connected to anxiety or worry are examined, they usually involve projected anxiety or concerns about past events yet anxiety is a "here and now" activity. It therefore stands to reason that anxiety is designed to offer solutions in the "here and now". After all no amount of worrying about a past event will change what actually happened. However, recognising the cause or steps that led up to whatever the past problem may have been allows us to take different steps in the "here and now" when we are faced with the same dilemma.

Again, this suggests that worrying is meant to be [and when used in the right way] a positive process. It allows us to identify poor actions or steps in the past that may have culminated in an unpleasant situation or event. This in turn allows us to avoid making the same mistakes.

"... true mammalian needs such as food, warmth, shelter, company, children, etc."

(Nice one Frank, just what I ordered! What more could this gorilla ask for?)

A similar situation applies to projected anxiety. Where this process is used positively potential pitfalls connected to a future event or situation can be identified and then avoided.

This very powerful procedure dramatically enhances our ability to meet our needs, giving us a very serious edge over other mammals.

Unfortunately, adapted needs are generally linked to emotions. This can be positive or negative i.e. love, hate, joy, sorrow, pleasure and pain etc.

It is in the pursuit of pleasurable emotions that where these are prevented or unachievable we become frustrated.

If you cannot avoid negative emotions [pain] then you begin to anxiete.

It is through these processes that worry/ anxiety becomes negative, generally causing as much if not more harm than the very things we cannot achieve or cannot avoid. Since there is rarely a solution the process generally deteriorates into depression or compensatory behaviour such as substance abuse, obsessive behaviour, over eating, aggression, etc.

It is important to ensure that your mammalian needs are not only met but are seen to remain safe and will continue to be met.

*It is also important to practice using the worry process **positively** by actively looking for causes _and_ solutions.*

Where the worry process is connected to adapted needs, then reminiscing (past) or fantasising (projected anxiety) can modify it. Whilst neither reminiscing or fantasising will normally fix the problem or offer a true solution, they are a far more beneficial process than anxieting over something that cannot be resolved.

In fact, many people do these things naturally in an *attempt* to improve their present position. Often this is the wrong way to use these two skills. Whenever we have a problem in the "here and now" we should use the worry process to identify a *solution* rather than using reminiscing/ fantasising to take our conscious mind away from our present situation. It is only where the object of anxiety is firmly fixed in the past or future and where it **cannot be resolved** should reminiscing/ fantasising be used.

Yet another reminder that it is one of the aims of this book that the knowledge in the book be used to improve our lives, in particular by assisting us to live in the "here and now" literally living each event as it comes.

Rather than a very poor but universal habit of constantly hopping mentally from the past to the future and back again.

Quality of life is always reduced when we focus our attention on to events in the past that could have been handled differently. Or when we focus our attention on to future events that may affect us in some negative way.

It is a <u>fact</u> that *regardless* of the position of our mind, our body must always continue in the present.

Therefore to gain the highest quality of life, both our activities and our minds should ideally be focused in the present. Contrary to popular belief we cannot effectively multi-task. We are most efficient when we carry out any one activity at any given time. By trying to carry out an activity in the "here and now" whilst allowing our minds to dwell on the past or wander forward into the future, reduces our efficiency/ involvement/ enjoyment/ etc. in the present.

CONCLUSION

On page one of this book W3M^{TM} I asked you to imagine a world where there is no war, no depression, little illness, where people are actually happy [as opposed to existing from day to day]. Neighbours are friendly, interested and not only have time for you, but will actually go out of their way to help. Crime, poverty, hunger, drug abuse are almost unheard of.

That was intended to be the world you live in now!

You may be wondering how these things would occur, or even how **you** can change some of the situations you have read in this book that actually affect you.

Quite simply! Just by *understanding* yourself better you now have choices. Having the *knowledge* of what and why, shows the path to learn "How to?".

Your Child mind may be hurting inappropriately, your Script/ s might be losing, your Stamp Books are full to overflowing, etc.
Since you now know you have a Child mind, Script, Stamp Book, you can begin to work with them. Perhaps you could reassure your Child or help it to learn to let inappropriate feelings go. Perhaps you could create a Counter Script, or you could break a driver supporting the Losing Script. Perhaps you could trade some of your stamps in a more positive way and stop collecting as many new stamps.

Any one of these **actions** would help improve the situation described above.
Yet you could not do <u>any</u> of these things, if you did not know that you had a Child mind/ Script/ Stamp Book?

When enough people understand and apply the contents of W3M^{TM} then things will change.

Parental judgements can be tempered with Adult understanding and reasoning; where criminals can <u>genuinely</u> be rehabilitated through **self-responsibility** and **understanding** <u>before</u> they are released back into the community.

This is not a soft option and there is no suggestion in this book that this should be a <u>replacement</u> for punishment, but that at the very least it should **accompany** punishment. But let us in our Adult minds recognise that the justice system today **is** a system of <u>punishment</u> **not** *rehabilitation.*

If a criminal offends through their Parent or Child minds, they are unlikely to recognise that their offence is anti social and unacceptable.

Punishing the Parent often brings two peculiar responses: -

The Parent mind may quite happily feel that it has more than paid for its offence in full and therefore the next offence should be punishment free.

Or even worse, the Parent mind may feel that it was *entitled* to carry out that offence and therefore the punishment system is unjust.

This may lead a criminal to carry out **more offences** to demonstrate: -

a. That they were in the right.

b. That the system is wrong.

c. That they should be compensated in some way for being wrongly punished in the first place.

Punishing the Child can also bring a peculiar response; that the Child mind feels that it only *wanted* something and hasn't really done any harm.

In fact, the Child may feel quite contrite and therefore feels that it shouldn't be punished at all. This builds up resentment and again the criminal may merely be biding their time until they can get even. This fails to address the vital issue that these particular Child "wants" are either inappropriate/ excessive/ unacceptable in Society.

If this is not **understood** by the <u>criminal</u> then they **will** continue to offend.

It is through understanding and recognition of the **consequences of our behaviour** that our behaviour can be modified.

Whilst this obviously does not <u>guarantee</u> that criminals will not re-offend, it can **reduce the likelihood** that they will not re-offend.

Far more importantly, it gives the criminal *alternative* choices.

If a true understanding and recognition of the **consequences**[*] of their behaviour is demonstrated by a criminal who then re-offends, it is at **this point** that they should suffer the full weight of the law.

Most drug abuse begins as a method of feeling different/getting away from reality. Sometimes we wish to just "feel good" or create an intense feeling of pleasure. Sometimes life sucks and we just want to switch off or chill out. Worse still, sometimes there is no point to life and drugs are an easy option. Sometimes with soft drugs we are fighting back against a perceived Parental society. <u>All</u> of these types of feelings can become habit forming and even so called non addictive recreational drugs can become habitual because of the driving need to meet or alleviate the above feelings. People that are happy, well-adjusted sharing and enjoying pleasures in life having reasons for living and hopefully direction in life, do not need to escape. For them, reality *is* a pleasure. Obviously, these happier people will still have ups and downs but life in general is good. Therefore habitual drug use is unnecessary. In addition to risk their happy fulfilling lifestyles through prosecution for drugs or drug related offences is unacceptable. However, in the former situation if there is no point to life, then you have nothing to lose and the threat of prosecution is unlikely to deter you.

* The consequences of the behaviour in recent terms has meant the punishment that, that behaviour will incur.

In W3M™ it is the **actual** consequences of their behaviour. The pensioner that spends the rest of their days in poverty/ fear/ pain because they were burgled or mugged. The family that is torn apart through the rape or murder of a family member. That it is not just the immediate victim that suffers from rape/ murder, but their entire family.

The corner shop serving a poor community, closes after one robbery too many, depriving hundreds of people of their community spirit and centre.

Not what *may* happen if they are caught? But what **actually** happens!
Again by helping drug abusers to understand themselves, to be able to recognise options and choices in life, to be able to move away from the sources of pain and unhappiness in their lives, will allow rehabilitation to be come an option.

However, weaning someone off drugs and then putting them back into the same environment that led them to use drugs in the first place, is pointless.

As with other criminals, self-responsibility and understanding is the first step to complete recovery.

But without something to make their previous activities pointless then they will struggle.

Society **itself** needs to become <u>Adult</u> to provide support for the under classes. (Political Correctness encourages Society to adopt Parental and Child responses. In particular where legislation is involved.)

Poverty in Western Society is a **reality** and no number of well-intentioned politicians trying to tell people otherwise will change that.

However, most poverty is self-inflicted. Sometimes through stupidity, mostly through ignorance. *

Again, by understanding and taking responsibility for our own actions we can prevent ourselves from suffering in poverty.

Whilst I am not suggesting that everyone suffering from poverty drinks, smokes and uses drugs, this is an easy example to show how quickly poverty can be created: -

Your weekly income is for argument's sake £/$200 a week.

* The word "ignorance" is used throughout W3M™ in its *proper* sense. I.e. Lack of knowledge. Rather than it's insulting or derogatory form.
As you can see from this demonstration, without taking into account any other expenditure (furniture, travelling, taxes, vehicle if you have one etc.) you are already £/$60 per week over your budget.

Your rent is £/$40, your electricity and gas average £/$20, with two small children your clothing bill averages £/$20, and your food/ household items average £/$60 per week.

You smoke £/$20 per week, you drink £/$80 per week and occasionally use £/$20 dope/ crack per week.

If you *react* in your Child mind, it is possible that you will attempt to save the money by cutting back on your food bill, clothing bill and by skipping rent.

Clearly both you and your children are living in poverty; you cannot afford new clothes, food often lacks nutritional value and you live in fear of your landlord.

It doesn't take a genius to realise that if you accept self-responsibility and understand the concepts offered in this book, then by over-riding your negative Child your situation will improve dramatically.

By stopping smoking, using dope/crack and cutting your alcohol bill down to £/$20 per week then you need no longer suffer in poverty.

In fact, you now have a spare £/$20 to go towards any other expenditure and/ or to provide more choice in your food and clothing bill.

Most poverty in Western Society is self-imposed.

It would have been just as easy to show the above example with a teetotaller, non-smoking, non drug-using parent who still inflicts poverty on themselves and/ or their family through debts (whether created through gambling or excessive expenditure incurring large loans or whatever).

This would still be self- imposed. There would still be choices.

The poverty could be avoided.

Occasionally poverty is inflicted through the Parent mind. Whilst there is good intent, the end result i.e. poverty is still the same.

This time our parent has a very low paid job.

Whilst there were two parents to support the family, things were not too bad but unfortunately the partner has left/ died/ whatever and one person is trying to bring up the two children on their own.

The total household income is £/$120 per week less £/$20 per week given to a neighbour for looking after the children.

This person is a paragon of virtue, no smoking, teetotaller, no drugs but again the figures still do not add up.

The rent is £/$40 the electricity and gas average £/$20, with two small children your clothing bill averages £/$20, and your food/household items average £/$60 per week. As you can see these figures overspend by £/$40.

Our hero/ine courageously cuts back on the food bill to try and keep within budget.

Lets face it you are hardly going to get a varied and nutritionally correct diet for a family of three on £/$20 a week.

Remember that this figure includes **all** of your purchases from the supermarket. Including cleaning materials, toiletries, toilet tissue, coffee, etc.
The figures given for the clothing allowance are small enough.

There isn't really any room for cutting back without inflicting hardship/ poverty on the family. Yet this person whilst they are in their Parent mind is unlikely to approach any welfare agency or appeal for additional state benefit.

Thoughts of duty, responsibility or even a believed intent that they should support the family are the kind of *drivers* that may push them into poverty.

As you may have already recognised, that where any of our examples had understood the issues in this book. And chosen to accept self-responsibility, therefore over-riding whichever process placed them in difficulty in the first place, then their lives and the lives of their families would improve accordingly.

However, it is the responsibility of Society to lend additional support in such a way that it helps the individual to fulfil their needs and capabilities.

Hopefully, these arguments will have helped you to accept that if the knowledge in this book is <u>understood</u> and <u>implemented</u> on a individual/ social/ national/ international scale it will eventually lead to the eradication of most crime and almost all poverty, hunger and drug abuse.

Ultimately, we really could live in a world without war or depression, little illness, where people are actually happy.

But before this can happen each and every one of us needs to understand ourselves and to accept responsibility for our own behaviour and actions.

For how can we expect society to implement something that we are not prepared to do ourselves?

If you *really* want a world where things are fairer, where relationships last, where people are happy, etc. then *you* need to change first!

Look after your own mental health, balance your minds, increase your Stroke generation, avoid Stamp Collecting, create Adult options/ choices, etc. In doing this you will feel happier, more in control of life; you will find yourself gaining the things you really want in life.

Your friends and family will become more comfortable with you; and as you get the life *you* want, so the people around you will want to learn about your success.

As they learn and hopefully put some of the ideas in this book into practise so their lives will change and they will pass that knowledge on to others. When enough people in any one area do this, then that particular area will change for the better.

Start **now**. Not tomorrow, not soon, not one day, start now!

Avoid negative phrases such as:- I'll try, I want to, but what about?, if only?, s/he has to first, etc.

All of these phrases are excuses!

When you say, "I'll try" your unconscious mind already expects you to fail!

"I want to" means I don't believe I can.

"But what about…." means you are looking for an excuse not to.

"If only" usually means you aren't even going to consider changing!

"S/ he has to first" means you are not accepting responsibility for yourself.

Everyone is unique; therefore readers that put this into practise will change their lives at a different pace.

Some readers will **literally** be enlightened and changes will begin almost immediately.

Other readers may take weeks before they see a change.

A few readers may take months before they see any changes.

Do not be disheartened **any** change that genuinely makes your life better and/ or makes you happier is worth putting the effort into.

Remember this is all new to you, so making the odd mistake along the way is to be expected. Also this is very much a "what is it" book rather than a "how to fix it" book; the clues to change are there but you may need to read each chapter a few times before you see them.

You may feel that some of these issues have been naive.

If this is the case then you may have misunderstood or ignored some of the concepts in this book.

We are *driven* through our unconscious Child and Parent minds.

We are *driven* by our Scripts.

We are *driven* to survive through the receipt of Strokes.

We allow our mammalian responses to over-ride rational thought.

If these issues are not understood and taken into account they cannot be changed or modified for any great length of time. It is only through accepting our strengths *and* weaknesses that we may continue to grow.

This book has been an introduction into some of the concepts of Transactional Analysis.

It has been designed as a taster, something that may give you an interest to delve deeper. Or something that you may accept at the level it is being offered yet still give you the opportunity to change.

Throughout the book, through the examples offered you may have recognised how to change, although you may have preferred some written instruction or steps on how to change. But a series of steps to create changes and modify inappropriate responses throughout the entire range of Transactional Analysis would have taken another book in its own right.

I hope you have found this book useful and obviously if there is sufficient response from both the sales of this book and people showing an interest in change, then next time I shall attempt to write a simple "how to" manual as opposed to this simple "what is" manual.

<u>GLOSSARY</u>

ACADEMIA: A derogatory term [in W3M[TM]] used to identify any academic process and it's hidden structure. In particular the process of **corruption** in academic circles [mostly at university level], where knowledge is sold out for prestige or financial gain and/ or complicated to make it appear more valuable. Where myths may be sold as absolute truths, and truth is dismissed as a myth, provided the University involved keeps its grants/ chair/ mystique/ etc.

ADULT: The Adult (capital A) denotes the third "human" mind; characteristics include the awareness of time, self awareness [conscious] and use of conceptual language.

CAGER: A particularly derogatory term used by the motorcycling community, when discussing car users. Like zoo animals their entire behaviour changes once they climb into their mobile cage. Becoming aggressive, uncaring and thoughtless. One of the top causes of injury and death to motorcyclists is *other* road users.

Some cages require 100,000% more glass, 1000% more metal, 700% more plastic, 300% more rubber to construct than the average motorbike, yet still only carry one or two occupants. In addition the average cage uses more fuel and oil than the average bike, takes up more space, both on the highway and to park. Not surprisingly many bikers have a low view of cagers.

CHILD: The Child (capital C) denotes one of the "mammalian" minds; characteristics include the ability to distinguish between different intensities of pain/ pleasure [both consciously and unconsciously], then convert these into drives [positive "I want"/ desires, negative "Flight" response of stress/ fear and anxiety].

CONCEPTUALLY/ CONCEPTUAL LANGUAGE: Within this book both of these phrases refer to the hidden words, ideas and meanings behind each original word. E.g. Door: hidden ideas include shapes, materials [such as wood, glass, metal, beads, PVC, etc.], positions [front, back, side, top, bottom, etc.], opening mechanisms [such as hinges, sliding channels, revolving, etc.], furniture [such as knobs, handles, hooks, finger plates, kick plates, etc.], colour schemes, etc.

There are millions/ billions of combinations of these "hidden" facts about doors, that we access every time that we use a door or think of a door. This is one of the abilities that allow us to be human.

CONTAMINATION: This is where Child/ Parent drives are misinterpreted as Adult, or although recognised as Child or Parent still over-ride the Adult mind. The latter condition is best described through phobias, where the Adult mind *knows* and reasons that the situation is harmless, yet the Child over-rides rational thought, leading to fear and panic.

DEMON: This is a negative, often destructive part of the Child mind; that plays freely, but with little or no concern for the damage or harm it may do. Where conscious awareness and the Persecuting Parent is involved, the Demon can be "gleefully vindictive".

DRIVER: Unconscious feelings/ desires, semiconscious images ideas/ phrases and feelings, conscious images statements and feelings that "drive" our behaviour. Drivers can easily over-ride conscious rational thought. Scripts are supported by Drivers. Mammalian impulses are usually "Driven".

FIGHT RESPONSE: This is the mammalian/ Parental response whilst under stress. The initial response is competitiveness but with sufficient pressure this will become an intense need for aggression, leading to physical action and/ or rage.

FIRST DEGREE: There are many situations in TA where different intensities are involved, these are usually referred to as degrees. There are usually three degrees, with first degree being the lightest or least affective. [Game Playing, Points of Commitment, Scripts, use different degrees.]

FLIGHT RESPONSE: This is the mammalian/ Child response whilst under stress. The initial response is fear leading to a need to escape or "run away". If the potential threat cannot be escaped then anxiety and excessive worrying may lead to depression.

FRAMES OF REFERENCE: Individual platforms used by all three minds to identify that which is "real" and that which isn't. Variations include **basic** [using the senses], **complex** [using reasoning within the Adult], **false** [using emotions to identify reality] and **fake** [using a platform such as science or religion to construct new realities].

GAME PLAYING: Game Playing refers to a process used to take from, or give Strokes to others. However in W3M™ the negative effects of Game Playing are explored. I.e. The taking, or theft of Strokes usually from those who are least capable of defending themselves.

INSIDIOUS: Progressing in a hidden way. I.e. "The loss of vision in my left eye, was the first I knew of this insidious disease. If only it could have been recognised earlier?". Often linked to unpleasant intent, when referring to human behaviour/ condition.

LIFE POSITIONS: Also known as the OK Positions. These are initially unconscious decisions in regard to our perceived value/ status. Where in early childhood the decision that we and/ or our parents are intrinsically good or bad [i.e. OK or Not OK]. Using the Adult mind and/ or therapy these positions can be re-written, usually for our benefit.

LITERAL LANGUAGE: Used by young children and other creatures. Where each grunt, squeak, howl, gesture, facial expression, action, etc. has just one meaning for that particular species. Many of these meanings are common between species. Many mammals perceive the showing of teeth and/ or staring at each other as gestures of aggression.

METAMORPHOSIS: A change of form, condition, purpose and/ or character. E.g. A caterpillar changing into a pupae, changing into a butterfly. Is going through metamorphosis twice.

OK POSITIONS: See Life Positions.

PARENT: The Parent (capital P) denotes one of the "mammalian" minds; characteristics include **unedited** moral, social, religious, ethical, etc. frameworks/ rules. Judgements are made using these and applied accordingly [often with little or no conscious awareness]. The Parent adopts the "Fight" response in stress.

PERSECUTOR: The Parent mind can be reduced into separate parts one of these being the *Persecutor*. As it sounds it usually "persecutes" both it's own Child and other peoples Child minds. Often found working in parallel with the *Rescuer* (Parent) and the *Victim* (Child) [occasionally stimulates the *Demon* (Child)].

PERTINENT: Relevant to. To the point.

PERVASIVENESS: Permeate, affect, spread into.
Often used in media, as an *emotive phrase* suggesting [evil] intent when used to describe the effect [and how far it reaches] of a new cult/ drug/ crime/ etc. on teenagers.

POINTS OF COMMITMENT: Points of Commitment (PoC) are unconscious decisions. Traditionally used to identify changes in relationships, PoC's are connected to all aspects of human behaviour. I.e. the unconscious mind on passing through a PoC, is now committed in every sense to it's new perspective, partner or project.

PONDER: Weigh mentally, think over and/ or consider.

PSEUDO-LEGITIMATE EXCUSE: These are common to the Parent and Child minds, being any reason to explain or justify behaviour. Where such behaviour is usually unreasonable and/ or only benefits the person using the excuse. Pseudo-legitimate excuses often leave an emotional charge/ residue in the person that it is being used against.

PSYCHE: Term used in Freudian analysis to indicate the mind. In Jungian analysis to indicate the whole of our being/ mind, the conscious **and** the unconscious combined.

RAISON D'ETRE: The original reason or cause for the existence [or continued existence] of a thing or cause. French for "the reason for being". This wonderful Gallic phrase doesn't have an Anglo substitute, so it slipped into popular use in "Artistic/ philosophical" circles. [In fact one could say that raison d'être is the raison d'être for raison d'être. Sorry, a poor pun, only attractive to sad intellectuals with nothing better to poke fun out of!]

RESCUER: The Rescuing Parent mind often "takes over", rescuing the Child in such a way that growth and learning are restricted, even discouraged. Negative emotional charges are built up in the Child until it feels and behaves like a *Victim*.

SCRIPT: The story line for life, written in early childhood, supported by gestures, body language, verbal language, actions and behaviour used in adult life particularly under pressure. Variations include Banal/ Boring, Hamartic/ Losing [in particular third degree Losing Script] and Winning Script.

SCRIPTER: A person actively involved in their Script; also used as a term [usually in a derogatory way] to denote someone whose direction/ choices in life are dictated through their Script.

SECOND DEGREE: A condition that affects not only the individual but also their family and friends. Although usually describing negative situations, degrees can be applied equally to positive situations. Second degree (negative) is usually kept hidden or secret. Chronic Second degree usually deteriorates into Third degree.

SHADOW: A Jungian term roughly equating to the repressed mammalian drives in the Child and Parent minds. The more we *shine* as [civilised] human beings, the clearer our mammalian *shadow* becomes. In the "Iceberg" illustration the *pure* white of the iceberg [consciousness] is *tainted* by shadow [repressed unconscious desire].

STAMP: An unconscious representation of owed emotional debt and/ or Strokes; coming in different intensities and values. Whenever we feel *obliged* to do something; regardless of whether that obligation is in our unconscious mind or an external obligation [i.e. Social requirement], we usually place a "Stamp" of that value in our unconscious "Stamp Book" with the intent of redeeming it at face value at some point in the future.

STROKE/ S: Strokes are used by the unconscious mind to measure/ identify its level of survival.

An excess of Strokes leads to intense feelings of well-being/ euphoria.

A deficit of Strokes leads to anxiety, depression, ill health, and even death.

STRUCTURAL ANALYSIS: A specific interest/ analysis of the Child, Parent and Adult. In particular their roles in transactions or personality.

THIRD DEGREE: Where negative can lead to illness, injury, court appearances, even death [although not always the death of the person in Third degree!]. Although rare in comparison with chronic situations, an acute Third degree response can lead to the above conditions in hours in a seemingly happy or well-balanced person. [I.e. Suicide or demands for a divorce, after the first marital argument.]

TRANSACTIONAL ANALYSIS (TA): The analysis of interactions between two or more people, with the primary interest being in Stroke exchange/ generation. Usually used in W3M^{TM} to mean the entire psychology as a whole.

VICTIM: A stance adopted in the Child mind where negative emotions build up to such a degree that this particular part of the Child mind will feel and act like a victim. So common in Western Society that hundreds of millions of people are silently and unconsciously waiting to be "rescued". In adults this builds up resentment that may be actualised or projected in destructive ways. Working in conjunction with the Persecutor and Rescuer, the Victim creates **emotional** *drivers* that feed Losing Scripts.

MOMENTS

In all of our lives at certain times there are moments.
Moments where an action, word, gesture or inaction will change
the course of our lives.
We cannot go back, there is no second chance.
It is these moments that *make* us.

To live our sad lives in bitterness or resentment,
Or to be happy and free; whatever.
These pivotal moments become our destiny (and that of our
families).
How often do we look back thinking "if only?"

Staying in careers we should have left long ago,
Or changing careers we should have stayed with!
We know whom we should have committed to,
We know the partner we should have left!

These pivotal moments give us the chance to *grow up*, to move
free from our childhood programming.
To move free from those that fail their moments, yet extort
others to avoid the moment... the decision.
Decisions... moments taking us toward or away from self-
responsibility; self-respect.
Avoid the moment, fear the pain, yet another dark stain.

As we falter then fail our moments, we fail ourselves, our
families.
We so easily forget past chances and like lemmings rush in our
thousands to death; ignoring, fearing, failing, again.
Yet amid all of this comes a **Moment**, such a moment that to
fail it, to avoid it; is to die.
To die yet exist; as we fail our very purpose in life!

Such a moment, a vast chasm in time, a second, a lifetime.
Where we know, we know in the depths of our hearts, our very being;
That this moment will affect the universe itself,
The very fabric and nature of our being.

I have met such moments.
As I back away, failed, avoided.
I remained a child,
Forever the fool!

Yet now a man.
For I have met such a moment, I did not fall back, nor did I hesitate.
No longer the same, perhaps no longer sane?
But the world is truly forever changed.

When your moment comes will you recognise it?
Will you fail?
You'll want to hesitate!
Even avoid it!

For it is the measure of a man to know;
To know and step forward regardless.
Changing forever the balance...
For good or evil, light or dark.

What if?
Will your life bring only one moment,
Or many?
To stand alone; light or dark?

Somewhere we know. We know but choose to forget;
That every word, each thought and action,
Is noted, stained forever
By our Spirit, our nature, the depths of unconsciousness.

Every lie, each deceit, betrayal,
No matter how small,
No matter how big,
A moment failed, a moment lost.

We are forever the sum of our lies or truths;
Since we are the sum of our moments.
Each lie we become less, each truth perhaps more.
A Spirit in balance, a soul in torment.

You are your moments, good or bad,
Big or small.
If you fail your moments,
How can you face the moment?

David Buchan

"All that evil needs to flourish, is good people to do nothing!"

A bastardisation of a similar quote credited to [but strangely not found in his writings?] Edmund Burke. 1729-1797.

W3M™ Support Groups

W3M^{TM} is not just about psychology, but about making **your world** a better place.

There is a temptation when reading a book to only see the immediate facts; in this case that W3M™ is an explanation of common sense psychology. At this level there are benefits from simply understanding ourselves and new ways to look at or deal with psychological problems.

What I would like you to also consider is the potential of W3M™ to radically change and improve our everyday lives. To recognise that you can use the issues in W3M™ to truly make your life easier.

How often do we look at early 1950's films where everyone works together and there is a strong sense of community spirit; and wish perhaps just fleetingly that it would be nice to have that again? Where everyone knows you, speaks to you, is truly interested in your life. Where if you are ill, or have family difficulties, or financial difficulties, etc. everyone will rally round and help. The kind of film that inspires us, moves us, even brings tears to our eyes. The kind of film that cynical uncaring people say "its just a film, real life isn't like that! in fact it wasn't even like that in those days!". Yet it can be like that, where people enjoy living, where life is easier, where a strong sense of community spirit invigorates us and we feel a common sense of purpose. All you have to do is find/ create your community. Honestly there is little more to it than that.

A community [in the sense that I'm offering] is not a collection of shops along a high street, its not a village, it isn't a group of houses around a community centre. In the UK today there are thousands of modern estates built around so called community centres where people don't even know their neighbours, let alone have any sense of community spirit.

A community is a group of people with a sense of belonging, a common purpose, bonding together over time. There is a rare almost ethereal essence that binds people together to bring them into a community.

If this is the kind of community you wish to belong to then you can actually create it. By setting up a W3M™ support group, you will begin to bring people together, people with a common purpose. This meets the second criteria of a community. With regular contact [even by post!] a sense of belonging will develop, meeting the first criteria. The third criteria: bonding together over time, will take time and careful management as the group learns to support both each member and the group itself.

The first thing you need to decide, is what will be your common purpose?

Will your support group have a financial goal? Will it create employment? Will it provide cheaper accommodation? Will it provide cheap holidays? Will it offer a 30% discount on the groups grocery bills? Will it bring people together that have a similar problems or needs? Will you set up a group of like-minded people to chat to?
Will your group provide one of these things, or all of these things?

You're doing the hard work, set up the type of support group *you* need/ want.
Set up the type of Support Group **you** need. If **you** need the group, you will put in the necessary effort to keep it going. Don't be discouraged it may be a while before people join your group. As the group grows you may no longer need it, use your Adult to identify the person that now needs the group the most and pass it on to them. Look for other things the group may need and incorporate those things into the meetings.

If you need to get out of a financial rut, perhaps you could set up a financial support group. If you have a hundred people in your group each of whom can put £/$40 per month into the funds, your group has £/$48,000 per year to invest. Carefully invested you can gain a better return for the group than each individual would get.

Or create a new company/ business that will supply your group [and local] needs; this can return several times the original investment. After all, you will have a minimum of one hundred regular customers. Many small businesses would appreciate a guaranteed hundred regular customers.

Perhaps when the total business is worth £/$10M realise your assets and return it to the group. If this takes ten years of continuous investment each member will have contributed £/$4,800; which is now worth £/$100,000.

I know the figures seem outlandish, how could you make £/$100,000 from £/$4,800? It's important to remember that your business will have £/$480,000 invested over the ten years, allowing the purchase of stock at premium discounts. Plus the regular custom of your local community, the hundred investors and their families.

Many small businesses start up with less than £/$25,000 **total** investment and are modestly successful; obviously starting up with a guaranteed annual investment of £/$48,000 will give your business a tremendous advantage.

Or keep going till the business is worth £/$100M; each original investor is now a millionaire! All for £/$40 per month and buying their daily/ weekly products from the group's business.

Perhaps you'd rather have guaranteed employment than be a millionaire. Using similar figures setting up a local business that keeps people employed wouldn't be too difficult.

What a wonderful idea! You could do the kind of work you enjoy, working in an environment that you enjoy, with a reasonable salary, feeling appreciated for your input and all for £40 per month.

Whilst it might seem strange paying to get the kind of work you would like, many of us quite happily pay extra to get the brand of coffee or tea that we prefer. So we already do this but on a much smaller scale.

I know that **I** would happily pay a small percentage of my income to **enjoy** going to work, to **feel** appreciated for that work, to do the kind of work I truly wish to do, etc. Besides, in a group of one hundred people the odds are that at least one person would want to be/ do accounts, catering, production, administration, delivery, engineering, etc.
Where there is more that one, then posts can be shared.

Many people will just want to go in, do their work and not be hassled; so most things will be covered. If there is something no one will do, hire someone from outside the group.

NB It will take several years before everyone in the group will be employed, a fair way of dealing with this is the ensure that the members that are not working in the group's business receive some kind of annual dividend or benefit from their investment.

If you need cheaper grocery bills, combining the ideas given earlier, your group could set up a private discount warehouse where the members receive a 35% discount on their weekly/ fortnightly shopping bills. Plus of course when you leave the group you get your share of the investment back!

Maybe you need a holiday, using the same figures by the second year your group could have purchased four small holiday cottages. Each member would now be entitled to a free holiday for two weeks with his or her family in the cottages, per annum. In four years time, a month's holiday per year with no accommodation charges. Plus when you choose to leave the group you get your share of the investment back. At the five-year stage the group may decide to increase the value of the investment by renting out surplus cottages. Wonderful you have a free month's holiday each year and each annual investment is doubling in value!

NB Make sure the organiser/ committee for a financial support group and the manager of the business you invest in, aren't running second or third degree Losing Scripts!

Or maybe you are lonely; setting up a small group with similar interests or circumstances, where you meet regularly wouldn't be that difficult. Although if it's **your** group, you'll probably have to do all the chasing and organising, but you also get to choose the venue or activity!

Please remember that W3M^{TM} is not just about psychology, but about making **your world** a better place.

The options are endless, create your own choices, make your own future. Don't go "cap in hand" to a company pleading for a job, only to be sacked when the company downsizes [sacked so someone else can make **even more profit!**]; then go "cap in hand" to yet another company.

Don't put up with it any longer; only *Losers* say, "that's just life", "that's the way things are", "you can't change the system", etc.

With a little bit of effort life can be easy, we can live instead of existing from day to day, we can be happier.

Remember the counselling and self-help concept: -

The more effort you put in to the things that you already do; the more you get, of what you've got!

If you want things to change, do something different.

If you want to set up a group to discuss/ explore the benefits of W3M™, then that is fine. If you only want to set up a group to use one aspect of W3M™ such as Points of Commitment or Stamp Collecting, that's also fine. [A support group for converting *Losers* into *Winners* is probably needed in every town or city.]

Perhaps you may want to set up a support group that will create a "community", or you may just want to join a group, all of these are fine.

At the end of the day, please remember that you can choose to do nothing or you can choose to do something. It's your life.

If you would like to set up a W3M™ Support Group please register the group with the publishers by writing to: -

SOSM Publishing
PO BOX 56
SWINDON
SN5 6LT

186